Christmas 1974
Joe & Heather,
   Merry Christmas,
      Bob & Sandra

ONTARIO TOWNS

RALPH GREENHILL
KEN MACPHERSON
DOUGLAS RICHARDSON

OBERON

To the memory of Verschoyle Benson Blake, 1899 - 1971

R.G. & K.R.M.

For my wife, our parents and their grandchildren

D.S.R.

23

PREFACE

This book is a successor, in a real sense, to *Rural Ontario* by Verschoyle Benson Blake and Ralph Greenhill, published in 1969 by the University of Toronto Press. *Ontario Towns* was initiated by the same authors, but Mr. Blake died in 1971 while the work was in progress. It is not, obviously, the book he would have written, but we should like to think that it remains true to the spirit of his intentions.

Again it has been necessary to be selective in presenting a survey of the better surviving examples of nineteenth-century buildings and streetscapes in the smaller towns of southern Ontario. We have deliberately omitted the cities from this survey, partly to impose a limitation on its scope, but also because the architectural expression in the large urban centres is different – both more sophisticated and on a larger scale. On the other hand, we have included some buildings in rural settings to give a more complete picture of the development of what might be called the Ontario style.

It is a collection which could have been refined indefinitely, but for our concern and sense of urgency; some of the buildings represented here have already been altered – pointlessly and brutally – or even demolished. The future of others is uncertain. The mutilation or destruction of buildings such as these all too often reflects poverty, if not bankruptcy, of imagination, rather than 'regrettable necessity.'

Our greatest debt is to the late Verscholyle Benson Blake, who helped to select more than half of the plates and wrote the first draft of the captions for most of these. We are particularly grateful to Miss Sybille Pantazzi for suggesting our collaboration, and to Miss Marion MacRae, William B. Dendy and Peter John Stokes, who made many helpful suggestions. We should also like to acknowledge the assistance of Miss M.E. Brown of the Fisher Rare Book Library, University of Toronto; Mrs. Carol Eayrs; Miss Edith Firth of the Metropolitan Toronto Central Library; Walter E. Langsam; Mrs. Roberta Fralick; Jim Milne; Don Nethery of the Education Centre Library, Toronto; Stephen A. Otto; Miss Sylvia Romanik; and Miss Margaret Van Every of the Ontario Archives. Finally, we must thank the Ontario Arts Council and the University of Toronto.

As was the case with *Rural Ontario*, this book is entirely a joint effort. It is, in fact, nearly impossible to disentangle the separate parts played by the writer, photographer and researcher in preparing it for publication, and we all share the responsibility for it.

D.S.R., R.G. & K.R.M.

7

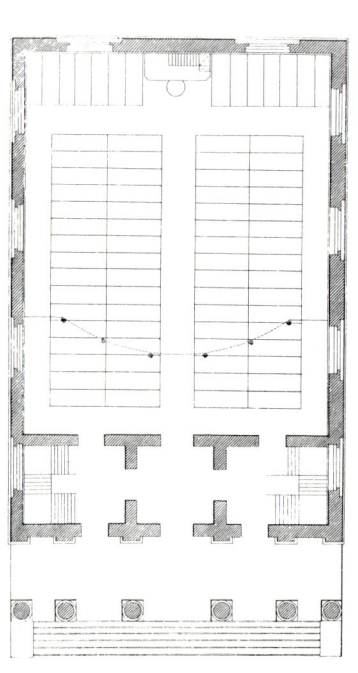

Fig. A.

Fig. B.

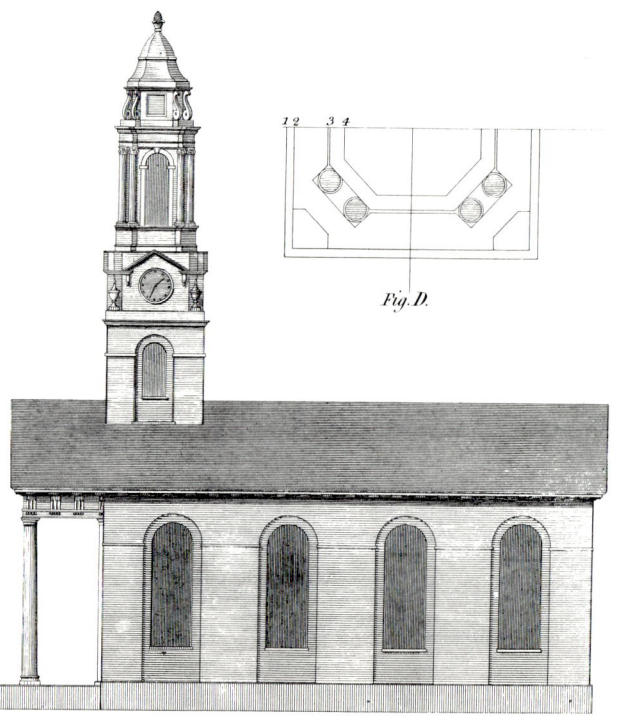

Fig. D.

Fig. C.

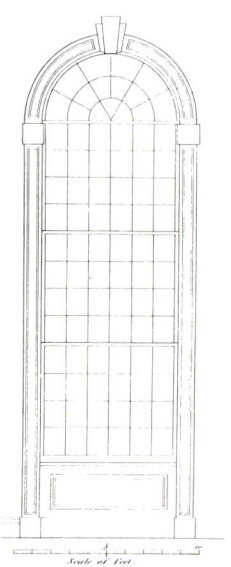

Fig. E.

HOUSES

At the beginning of this century Ontario's smaller communities possessed charm yet strength, variety and yet a sense of order—more than just a patina developed over long years of measured growth, they had real character. Many of these towns and villages, by-passed by the super-highway, still retain these qualities and have, until recently, escaped the wholesale ravages of modern development, though not its blight. Their buildings provide us with a sense of stability and tradition.

This tradition is not, however, of a highly stylized order; in the houses of the province, no architectural style is found in a form that could be considered very developed, or very advanced, except in the sophisticated urban centres. Even in the leading cities, Canadian architecture was never subject to the constantly-changing fashion typical of much American and European architecture in the nineteenth century. The American architect Asher Benjamin, in the preface to *The Practical House Carpenter* (Boston, 1830), noted that 'Since my last publication [which had appeared sixteen years before], the Roman school of architecture has been entirely changed for Grecian'; there was never anything like the same quality of fashionable change here.

The other side of the coin is that any feature or element of high style that did make an appearance tended to enjoy a long life, during which it achieved a kind of currency—alongside very disparate forms—that had little to do with the normal conventions of that style.

Several examples illustrate the extended life of isolated elements of style and the eclectic mixing of these in Ontario. The Barnum house at Grafton, built about 1819 (PLATE 7), is such an individual structure that it might be expected to be unique. One can find parallels for the distinctive arcaded treatment of the principal facade in upstate New York—none more handsome, nor any earlier—and one can find British counterparts of this sort of arcading (derived from mid-eighteenth-century work in brick or stone) published well into the nineteenth century.[1] But on Church Street in Colborne there is another handsome house, nearly a replica of the Barnum house at a superficial glance, which—to judge from the differing detailing—must date from the third quarter of the nineteenth century, fully 50 years after the Barnum model.

A superbly effective ensemble—one might almost say mélange—of separate stylistic elements is the large Bentley house in Brougham (PLATE 58): Georgian carcass, Neo-classical entrance with free-standing columns, Gothic Revival second-floor window with switchline tracery, classicizing and also gothicizing patterned brickwork at the corners and eaves, Italianate cornice and belvedere, and so on. But what is more remarkable than such a catalogue of individual elements, or even the high quality of execution of any of these, is the coherence with which all these rhythmically varied forms mesh to create a harmonious work of significance with a real sense of presence.

This confusing simultaneity of styles in nineteenth-century Canada prevailed in the world of sartorial fashion as well as architectural taste. Lower quotes a description in 1804 of a society ball at Kingston: 'Among the ladies . . ., the young ones, the present exaggerated Grecian costume was further exaggerated, with the addition of cropped heads, and waists between the shoulders. Some of their elders . . . rejoiced in imitation court dresses of half a century before: long-waisted stiff silk gowns, open in front, with lace . . . aprons; high-heeled shoes, and their powdered hair rolled over huge toupees stuffed with wool . . . Some beaux . . . had swallow-tailed coats, others the broad skirts of the days of William III.'[2]

Comparable differences are found in Ontario between neighbouring structures of related date; discrepancies are even found cheek by jowl within the same building. In satisfying compositions of high style elsewhere, uniformity of underlying principle normally accounts for the high degree of coherence from part to part. However, the concept of a consistent, let alone homogeneous approach to style, surface treatment, or detailing is almost irrelevant in the context of basically vernacular material.

It follows that stylistic analysis and stylistic grouping of the traditional sort may not be helpful; it may even be downright misleading. What is more important than any correspondence to a metropolitan sense of style is the actual quality in abstract terms of the work itself.

However, an awareness of related patterns in other places or at other times is essential to an understanding of our own position. As far as one can tell from the small number of our earliest buildings which survive, settlers in Ontario followed a variety of patterns from the beginning. Some building conventions were transplanted from the United Kingdom, others were brought upriver from Quebec, but the majority came from the recently established United States of America. In any case, these conventions were as natural to their builders as their mother tongue. But under the influence of so many architectural dialects—to extend the metaphor—it is not surprising to find many differently-accented buildings. In fact, many of the resulting architectural patterns are as distinctive and as localized as regional patterns of speech.

Superficially, the Matheson house of 1840 in Perth (PLATE 31) could almost pass for an American house of the previous century. A symmetrical house with a slightly-projecting central section under a broad gable, it is distantly related to houses of the grander sort in New England or the middle colonies in the third quarter of the eighteenth century. Only the elliptical fanlight over the entrance gives away the much later date of the house in Perth. But with its sparse detailing it is also simpler than the houses of Massachusetts, Pennsylvania or Maryland. And it is on a much smaller scale than comparable houses in the American colonies (even the small frame mansions of New England). The stone-masonry, however, is much more sophisticated than that found in the pre-Revolutionary states (where stone construction was rare outside Pennsylvania). In the Matheson house, the rubble stone is roughly dressed to rectangular blocks and there are smoothly-dressed stones not only in the keyed window-heads but also in the jambs of the windows and door, as well as in the quoins at the corners of the house. These dressed stones, regular in dimension, are aligned horizontally and made to touch, or nearly touch, in bands across the face of the house in a way that is distinctive of some Ontario stonework.

The reasons for similarities between such Canadian houses as this, or the Alpheus Jones house in Prescott (PLATE 16) and earlier American parallels—despite large differences in date—are probably two: first, the reliance on common British traditions; and second, the influx of American Loyalists into Canada at the close of the wars—the Revolutionary War and the War of 1812. However, the assumption that British tradition underlies both American and Canadian architecture needs more extensive examination of vernacular architecture in the United Kingdom to prove the close relationships.[3]

English architectural pattern books of the eighteenth century were less important as transmitters of the British tradition, even in the American colonies, than is sometimes suggested; most of the designs illustrated in such books are irrelevant in North America, especially in Ontario. Benjamin pointed out in the preface to *The American Builder's Companion* (Boston, 1806) that 'not more than one third of the contents of the European publications on this subject are of any use to the American artist in directing him in the practical part of his business,' because 'The style of building in this country differs very considerably from that of Great Britain, and other countries in Europe . . ., partly in consequence of the more liberal appropriations made for building in those countries, and . . . the difference of materials used.'

But rarely, as Isaac Ware's book, *A Complete Body of Architecture* (London, 1756), one finds a comparatively unpretentious design, like the Parsonage House in Yorkshire (fig. 1), which is helpful. The plan and elevation may both be compared with the Matheson house in Perth, if one ignores certain elements like the high wall or screen, the flanking stable and studio, and the fact that the kitchen and wash house are treated as one-storey sheds in Ware's design. Ware's book is known to have been available in some American libraries; whether or not it was available in Canada, similar basic patterns had already been established in the older territory south of the border, and could be recalled. Ware himself had commended conservative domestic design, feeling that 'more variety may be introduced than there is at present, but not so much as some have imagined.'[4]

Such traditional patterns could be adapted to different conditions of climate and geography. The economic and social reasons for departures from either the American or British precedents are equally interesting. The small size of the Matheson house might be taken as characteristic of Ontario. The rawness of the province—only beginning to be settled at the end of the eighteenth century—and the modest financial status of even the leading colonists must have been primary influences. The social fabric was also very different with regard to domestic help, and must have tended to encourage relatively smaller houses. Slaves were rare; as early as 1793 the Lieutenant Governor had instigated unique legislation which abolished the trade. As Charles Stuart's book, *The Emigrant's Guide to Upper Canada* (London, 1820) was quick to point out: 'The want of servants in Upper Canada is perhaps the greatest inconvenience to which persons of property are exposed.'[5] Finally, the severity of winter confirmed the wisdom of housing which was compact and easily heated. The English tradition of planning symmetrically paired outbuildings to flank the house, although imitated in the American middle colonies, was obviously inappropriate under such conditions. In Ontario, dependencies were grouped in a tail or ell at the rear of the building, largely hidden from view by the width of the house front, as in northern New England.

The superior workmanship in stone represented by the Matheson house can be accounted for in several ways. The abundance of good building stone lent itself to the development of masonry as a relatively common building technique (even if it made for difficult farming in many areas). The Harris house in Perth was built in 1823 by obviously competent masons (PLATE 30). Four years later the Rideau Canal was begun by the Royal Engineers, supported by large numbers of extraordinarily skil-

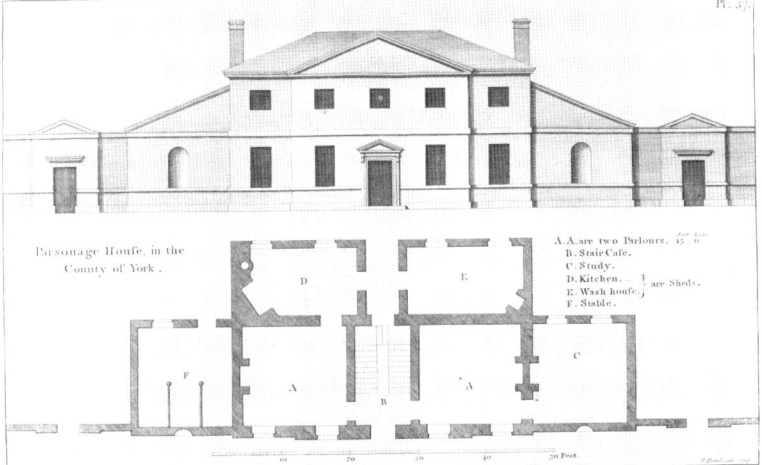

1

ful masons. The canal was an awesome feat of engineering and superlatively constructed. It gave new impetus to the town of Perth, among others, and to masonry construction in the area.

In spite of the excellence of its masonry, however, the Matheson house is severely plain, like the bulk of houses in this province, whatever the material, nearly to the end of the nineteenth century. One may contrast such buildings with the riches of more remote but hardly more populous British colonies like Tasmania. The extraordinary abundance of carefully-studied, intricately-detailed and gracefully-worked Tasmanian buildings—largely of stone—results partly, however, from two unique factors: the penal colony was in a position to command the talents of several skilled architects and numerous craftsmen; and abundant quantities of easily-worked stone of high quality were readily available and cheap.[6] Our resources in Ontario, material and personal, were of another order.

The materials in common use throughout the province were log, frame construction with a wooden cladding, stone and brick, probably in that sequence. But the least common materials in the early years of the province, stone and brick, are the most easily documented. The Manor, a stone house at Wellington in Prince Edward County, may possibly date from 1789 and would appear to be the earliest such structure surviving.[7] Three years later, in 1792, when John Graves Simcoe took office as the first Lieutenant Governor of the Province of Upper Canada, his wife commented: 'Kingston is . . . a small town of about fifty wooden houses and merchants' storehouses. Only one house is built of stone.' This house had just been built that year. Likewise, Mrs. Simcoe noted but one stone house of 1792 in Newark (Niagara-on-the-Lake), the capital.[8] In a petition the following year, William Dickson of Newark asserted that he had built the first brick house in the province, though its date is unclear.[9] However, most of the houses in the many sketches made by Mrs. Simcoe were evidently of clapboard over a heavy frame of square-hewn members—a form of construction which elicited no comment from her. The Simcoe's own residence at Newark was of log—part of a cluster of four such buildings known as Navy Hall (one of which was rebuilt in recent years as a stone structure).

The precedents for log construction in Ontario are undoubtedly American, although there were peculiarly French antecedents in this province. The notion that all the earliest settlers in the eastern part of this continent lived in houses built of notched logs was exploded many years ago by Harold R. Shurtleff in *The Log Cabin Myth*. But by the middle of the eighteenth century this mode of construction had been transmitted, evidently from Scandinavia via the Delaware basin, to the frontier territories, including those across the border from what would become Ontario, in the areas now known as western New York, northern Pennsylvania and Ohio, and it was carried into the province by early settlers removing from these or more remote frontier areas. The French also had forms of log construction, distinguished by grooved vertically-mounted members (at the corners and framing, between the openings for the windows and doors), but it seems that the few examples of these in Ontario which survived into this century were covered with siding, obscuring their identity until they were demolished.

The term log cabin—which didn't come into use until the nineteenth century—is used too broadly today; a distinction should be drawn among three different types of buildings: the shanty, the cabin and the log house. The differences have to do with the intended function and life-span of the structure, and its method of construction, size and finish.

The shanty was a makeshift, intended for temporary shelter only. It was small, undivided internally and crudely constructed, with low walls of untrimmed logs, generally with a shed roof of overlapping, split and hollowed logs, a dirt floor and one window at best—utterly without distinction.[10] A stereograph of the 1860s' identified by the photographer as the first settler's shanty in Palmerston, is reproduced here (fig. 2). As the first settler, Thomas McDowell, was granted land just south of Palmerston in 1862, the shanties illustrated in the view must date from 1862 or 1863. Such structures must have been built in large numbers but inevitably decayed quickly.

At the other extreme is the log house as ambitious in scale and design as a masonry house. The Priory, built in 1827 for John Galt, the Superintendent of the Canada Company, was such a building, though it later became a railway station (fig. 3). The design is that of a traditional masonry house and in general follows Isaac Ware's Parsonage House (fig. 1) even more closely than the Matheson house in that it has shed-roofed wings at either end. The Priory was the first house in Guelph but was destroyed in the 1920s (about the time of its centenary); the distinctive pattern was preserved, however, in a small log house on Palmer Street (PLATE 3). Such log houses were usually covered with clapboard, adding a skin to the chinked logs, as much to prolong their life and protect against drafts as for any aesthetic reason. In this instance, however, the use of exposed log may well have been conscious expression of materials and also self-expression: it was Galt who rhapsodized over the first tree cut on the site of Guelph (immediately beside his house, as it turned out): 'a large maple tree was chosen; on which, taking an axe from one of the woodmen, I struck the first stroke. To me at

2

least the moment was impressive – and the silence of the woods, that echoed to the sound, was as the sigh of the solemn genius of the wilderness departing for ever.... The tree fell with a crash of accumulating thunder ... [and] there was a funereal pause, as when the coffin is lowered into the grave.'[11] Surely for Galt the use of log had a special value, and represented a sophisticated appreciation of a primitive material.

Between the shanty and log house is the log cabin, a type generally of storey-and-a-half design, nearly symmetrical, relatively modest in size, and closely similar to the masonry houses known as cottages, but for the fact that the interior of the log cabin was sometimes undivided. More permanent than a shanty, many of these must have been intended to meet the requirement for 'a good and sufficient dwelling house' measuring at least sixteen by twenty feet, to be built within the first year after taking up land. This regulation was part of the list of improvements constituting settlement duty which were made uniform in 1798. More than half a century later a 'Notice to Settlers' was published which still required a house (at least twenty by eighteen feet) as a condition of settlement, but was quick to point out that 'the Log-house required by the Government to be built is of such a description as can be put up in four days by five men. The neighbours generally help to build the Log-cabin for newly arrived settlers, without charge ... the roof can be covered with bark, and the spaces between the logs plastered with clay, and white-washed. It then becomes a neat dwelling, and warm as a stone house.'[12]

Through most of the nineteenth century the front door was the one feature of Ontario houses to sustain much elaboration. In the early examples, until the period immediately after the War of 1812, the doorway was not particularly wide. It was commonly topped by a semi-circular transom or fanlight, often within a square-headed frame provided by extending the doorcase, though in its simplest form, the transom was rectangular, as in the log house in Guelph (PLATE 3).

The door treatment in the Barnum house at Grafton (PLATE 7) is unusual for this province: it preserves the English mid-Georgian fashion of setting the transom within a small gable or pediment, but the window is, in fact, a dummy, with real mouldings applied to a panel which is painted black to look like glass.[13]

A wider and bolder entrance became fashionable soon after the War. Sidelights were added flanking the door and providing much more light for the hall, as in the house at 83 Gage Street in Niagara-on-the-Lake (PLATE 10); here, atypically, the transom is omitted. It was customary to make the various elements cohere by encasing them all – door, transom and sidelights—with mouldings, as in the Spencer house of the 1820s, in Cobourg (PLATE 6). This house has an entrance which is further articulated by an all-too-rare example of an early porch with slender columns spaced to match the rhythm of door and sidelights, and comparable pilasters acting as responds to frame the windows and door.

The practice of extending the transom laterally over the sidelights is less sound structurally, but a very pleasing arrangement and a typical pattern in Ontario. This form shows clearly in the Macpherson house at Napanee (PLATE 5), though the loss of the porches on both sides of the house—leaving only the pilasters to either side of the doorcase—creates an impression of incompleteness.

The most common form of transom in Ontario from the 1820s into the 1840s, a fanlight crowning both door and sidelights, is only one of many entrance treatments found in contemporary American practice. This type is particularly effective, whether simplified with plain mouldings and straightforward glazing bars or muntins, as in the Matheson house at Perth (PLATE 31), or embellished with carved capitals in the doorcase and festooned with swags and cast-lead ornaments in the transom, as in the Breakenridge house at Niagara-on-the-Lake (PLATE 11). The fanlight over sidelights originated in Britain and was associated especially with Robert Adam, but was given a distinctive twist in North America. For even in Adam's latest work, in the closing decade of the eighteenth century, the transom is either a half-circle or segmental, but in Ontario, the fanlight is almost invariably elliptical.[14]

The reason for the elliptical form of the Ontario fanlight was undoubtedly related to the climate. Heating a building in winter from a few open hearths was a problem in Ontario, and encouraged the construction of houses which were compactly arranged: the British and European taste for very tall rooms was impractical here. Down to the middle of the nineteenth century, ceiling heights of more than eight and a half or nine feet are rarely encountered in houses outside centres like Kingston and Toronto, and even there such heights were uncommon. It would have been difficult to fit a truly semi-circular transom over a door within the headroom available and quite impossible to do so if the fanlight were to embrace the sidelights as well.

One type of house, which gained favour in the first quarter of the nineteenth century and continued far into the third quarter, has since been dubbed—rather misleadingly—the Ontario cottage. Here the term cottage refers to a type which is by no means unique to Ontario, but is found throughout the English-speaking world—with the important exception of the United

3

States, where it is rarely encountered. This type of cottage, wherever it occurs, is generally distinguished by its long, rectangular form, its single-storey appearance, and its low-pitched roof sloping in from all four sides (technically a hipped roof). It is generally a small building, but in Ontario practice the cottage may, on occasion, be raised above the ground with a high basement, or may even have another storey concealed in the attic. By mid-century, such cottages were sometimes given a small, short, glazed superstructure—called a lantern or monitor—to light the attic space, as in the farmhouse near Allisonville, in Prince Edward County (PLATE 61). Both the hipped roof and the monitor might, of course, also be found on two-storey houses, as in the Bentley house at Brougham [PLATE 62].

As distinct from the Ontario cottage, the typical Ontario house is a storey-and-a-half affair, gable-roofed, and taller in appearance. The upper storey is often visible only in the end walls. In the gable ends, the upper windows are frequently smaller than the ground-floor windows, and more closely spaced to fit beneath the raking eaves.

The popularity of the storey-and-a-half house with tall front and rear walls was largely due to a peculiarity of Upper Canada taxation. An act of the legislature in 1807 classified houses for taxing purposes according to the number of storeys, as well as the material of which the building was constructed and the number of fireplaces it contained. The act 'served to increase the popularity of the storey-and-a-half house, and to make it the usual type of farm dwelling in this province [and a type to vie with two-storey houses in villages and towns]. A full upper storey increased the cost of construction, especially where the walls were of brick or stone, but this might not have offset the inconveniences of these early attics, scant of head room, inadequately lighted and ventilated, roasting hot in summer and, before stoves became common, often cold in winter. That these inconveniences were felt is clear from the tendency to heighten the walls to the eaves, to enlarge the gable windows as chimney flues became fewer and smaller, and to insert small windows under the eaves almost at the floor . . . . However, the fact that a house of less than two storeys paid appreciably less tax than a house of two storeys with the same superficial area and the same number of rooms, and that this disparity increased with each additional fireplace, certainly influenced some settlers to decide to forego the added comfort and superior status . . . of a house of two full storeys.'[15]

In the characteristic storey-and-a-half house, the space between the heads of the ground-floor windows and the horizontal eaves is punctuated by a centrally-located opening used to light the upper hall. These openings took a variety of forms. In the Port Hope area, for example, a small, semi-circular window with no gable was a favourite. Along the Rideau, a broad, low gable was used. Sometimes the gable was a later addition, which accounts for its more acute form in the Harris house at Perth (PLATE 30).[16] A square, three-part window with a centre light wider than the flanking lights is found in eastern Ontario, while a window with an elliptical head—usually matching the doorcase—is found along the St. Lawrence. Ultimately the gable became very acute and the Gothic window with its pointed head—or the Tuscan with its round head—appeared everywhere.

A common but perishable feature of both the Ontario cottage and the storey-and-a-half house was the veranda—also employed to effect in larger houses like that designed by Kivas Tully for Charles Jones of Weston in 1854 (fig. 4). The veranda has a particularly complex architectural history. A feature of vernacular architecture in northern Portugal, it was exported to Brazil, the West Indies and Portugal's eastern colonies before the end of the seventeenth century. Spreading into British possessions, it became popular in sophisticated English circles late in the eighteenth century and early in the nineteenth under the influence of the Prince Regent. It was particularly common in South Africa and both one and two-storey houses with this feature are known there as veranda houses.[17] Although John Plaw gave prominence to an 'American Cottage' with a veranda on three sides in his book of designs, *Ferme Ornée* (London, 1795), the veranda is, in fact, relatively rare in American practice, with the exception of Gothic Revival villas of the mid-century.[18] The American piazza, which was comparable in function but not in form, consisted of a substantial covered area with a nearly horizontal roof supported by classicizing pillars, and was commonly applied to the ends of the house. In spite of its vaguely architectonic form, such a porch was rarely an important visual element.[19] By contrast, the veranda was a slight thing structurally, but generally extended the length of the principal face of the building, frequently running down one or both sides, and sometimes completely encircling the house (as originally at Riverest in L'Orignal [PLATE 28]). It created a deeply shaded area against which the pattern of strongly-lit supports at the leading edge played effectively and rhythmically, so that it became an important organizing element of the design.

In Britain, veranda supports were commonly wrought-iron panels, with a web of elements between relatively thin verticals at the outer edge of each panel; this treillage form was adapted to wood—a much weaker medium—in Ontario. Only a few

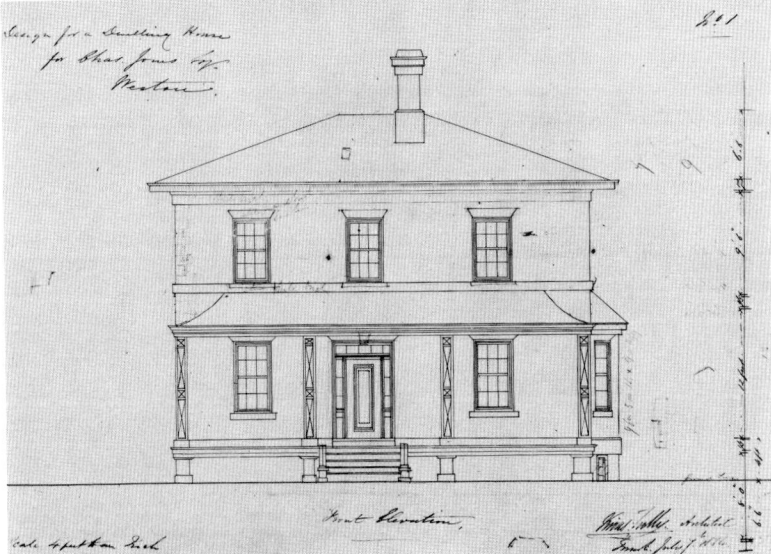

well-cared-for or stout specimens of treillage survive. Most remaining Ontario verandas of early date were constructed with simple posts; turned posts, however, became common in the 1860s. Frequently the supports—whether treillage or posts—were supplemented by elliptical arcading as in the house on Mill Street in Elora (PLATE 64), though few examples were as substantial as this. Here, as in Tully's design, the veranda roof was carried on curved rafters to produce the bell-cast curve—a tent-like form suggesting impermanence, no matter how robustly executed the veranda might be.

The break between veranda and house is strong in Ontario, as in the farm house near Stouffville (PLATE 63), and stresses the horizontal elements of the structure—those parallel to the landscape. Only in some early examples of the Ontario cottage was the veranda roof continuous with the roof of the house itself, as in the cottages of the southern hemisphere, which play up the sheltering form of the building. The many houses in this province from which verandas have been removed (PLATES 10 and 61) have not only lost a useful element and acquired a somewhat severe appearance, they have also become detached to some degree from their setting, functionally and visually.

Despite the ingratiating quality of the house with a veranda, much Ontario architecture is distinguished (as already suggested) by its inordinate plainness and its apparent independence, and these characteristics—especially noticeable in our stone buildings—probably owe much to the high degree of Scottish influence in this province. Perth, heavily settled by Scots, is a fine example of a stone-built town (PLATES 30, 34, 73 and 77), and its buildings seem to reflect the impact of Scottish temperament on the emergent Ontario personality. Civil to a degree, but straightforward and even blunt, Canadian character was repeatedly remarked by early observers for a directness which bordered on boldness.

But the dourness of Ontario masonry, at least, is equally attributable to the stone of which our buildings are constructed. Andrew Bell, who was active in 'engineering and architectural building' throughout the latter half of the nineteenth century, commented on the 'great variety of valuable, useful and ornamental building stones, in unlimited quantities, for almost any purpose in building, except for highly ornamental cutting such as can be done with the Ohio and similar free stones—of that there may be said to be none or next to none.' Ontario—eastern Ontario especially—abounds instead in granite, coarsely crystallized marble, and a coarse-grained sandstone, but above all in what Bell called 'Trenton group' limestone. Blue limestone was more commonly used throughout the province than any other building stone, including grey limestone. Fine-grained, breaking sharply into blocks, the former has two real disadvantages: 'The "Blue" is generally bright in appearance when first quarried, but unfortunately fades in a few years and becomes a "sickly" white, as may be seen at Kingston and other places.' Moreover, 'It does not cut nearly so well as the grey.'[20]

In other words, our commonest building stone was readily available but tolerated a limited range of form. A sensitive architect like George Browne of Kingston (who also practised at Quebec and Montreal) might use the material sympathetically in a big building like Kingston City Hall by arranging it in large planes but making only a minimal attempt at tooling or texturing the stone. In smaller structures one could only depend on the building's massing—as Kivas Tully did in his very effective Christ Church, Lakefield (PLATE 47). Significantly, both Browne and Tully were Irishmen, and had learned to cope with the scarcely more tractable limestone and granite which constitute the principal building materials of Ireland.

Not very surprisingly, therefore, the most self-conscious building stylistically in a stone town like Perth is not of stone, but of brick: the MacMartin house, begun 1830 (fig. 5 and right side of PLATE 33). Daniel MacMartin was a lawyer of Loyalist stock and American training, who met the antagonism of local British half-pay officers by building the largest and most ambitious house in town. For his pains, he was dubbed Haughty Mac, but his house remains the finest example of its sort in the province. It represents a North American interpretation of later eighteenth-century British style. The analogous manner in the United States about the turn of the century is described as Federal style; imported into Canada from the United States at a still later date, the Ontario variant of this distinctive style has properly been called Loyalist. The daguerreotype, made about 1850, not long after the house was built, shows how little it has been altered in the intervening years.

The MacMartin house boasts all the refinements of Loyalist style. Though it is a brick house, it has a full complement of stone trim. It has stone quoins at the corners, stone lintels with keystones as well as stone sills on the windows, a stone stringcourse between the storeys, a stone cornice at the eaves, and a marble doorcase (with an elliptical fanlight) originally approached by a high flight of stone steps. The roof is hipped, with a vented cupola in the centre, originally flanked by matching but smaller lanterns to light the attic storey. The front wall with its large windows is treated as one shallow, arcaded plane thinly masking another, as in the brick house on Queen Street in Niagara-on-the-Lake (PLATE 12) or the Barnum house at Graf-

5

ton (PLATE 7), both approximately ten years earlier. The mouldings of the MacMartin house are consistent with its Loyalist idiom: 'extremely linear, knife-edged and complex.'[21] But the chunky proportions of the house as a whole, and the heavy—even gouty—classicism of the fluted piers in the doorcase (as well as the interesting Greek Revival decor inside) distinguish Canadian Loyalist work—and this house in particular—from American Federal work.

Robustly-handled classicizing detail is peculiarly associated with the Greek Revival and an indication of continuing American influence. But this mode—characterized by large orders generally executed in wood—was rarely adopted wholeheartedly in this province.

The plain but very substantial brick houses with Greek Revival accents, which were built around the middle of the century, are the most deeply satisfying of all Ontario houses in this genre. In the Sovereign house of 1842 in Waterford (PLATE 43), the plainness of Ontario taste is entirely in accord with the reticence of that mature phase of classicism in which simple detailing, large scale and a sense of full form combine to make a strong statement. The deep and strongly projecting cornice emphasizes the mass of the house. Even the porches of such houses convey a pleasurable sense of solidity (PLATE 41).

Until the middle of the nineteenth century, Ontario builders made little use of pattern books; not even leading architects had much in their libraries that was particularly relevant. For example, John G. Howard (1803-90), Toronto's first City Surveyor, who had emigrated from England in 1832 and later left his remarkable library to the city, seems to have had relatively few architectural books.[22] On the other hand, most of the books belonging to Frederick W. Cumberland (1821-81) who emigrated to Toronto in 1847, are characteristic of the much more specialized British publications of the 1840s and 1850s, and could have been useful only in the modish milieu of the provincial capital.[23]

Virtually nothing originated or was published here on the subject of domestic architecture until the *Canada Farmer* made its appearance in 1864. The solitary exception in this field was a little-known but important technical work by the Canadian engineer, Henry Ruttan, *Ventilation and Warming of Buildings* (New York, 1862); Ruttan lived in Cobourg, and dedicated his book to the Governor General although it was published in the United States.[24]

Meanwhile, Ontario architecture was much influenced by the many new American pattern books which appeared around mid-century. These were less technical yet more comprehensive than earlier books, and generally contained a longer text, which was directed at the client at least as much as the architect. Of the scores of titles, some of the most popular ran through many editions and tens of thousands of copies over a long period of time; the most influential was undoubtedly A.J. Downing's *Cottage Residences* (New York, 1842), a new edition of which was released in 1887 – following a dozen other editions or revisions – 45 years after the first![25] The emphasis in the titles of this and other works, like Downing's *The Architecture of Country Houses* (New York, 1850), or Calvert Vaux's *Villas and Cottages* (New York, 1857), is on houses intended for a suburban or rural locale. Unlike earlier treatises, these new books were aimed at an expanding middle class. They answered a real need for a practical guide that would illustrate recent trends applicable to a free-standing house of relatively modest size.

The type borrowed from American pattern books which is most readily identified is the octagonal house. It originated with the New York phrenologist Orson S. Fowler, who published a very popular illustrated work entitled *A Home for All; or, the Gravel Wall and Octagon Mode of Building* (New York, 1848). The book was intended to demonstrate two things: the advantages of concrete and, as the wordy subtitle makes clear, the application of this newly-rediscovered building material to buildings of octagonal shape, whether small or large, because of 'the capacity, beauty, compactness and utility of octagonal houses' compared with the 'defects in small, low, long-winged, and cottage houses.' Fowler recommended concrete as being strong, readily available, inexpensive, and calculated to maintain even temperatures. As for the octagonal shape, it was close to the most compact form, the circle, and therefore enclosed the maximum space with the minimum wall. If the internal planning posed problems, Fowler thought it also offered an opportunity to apply the 'universal law of progress' to house-building in order to achieve a 'radical improvement,' chiefly by the elimination of much hall space, the re-ordering of circulation through the house, and the reduction in heating cost in such a building.

The small octagonal house at Picton (PLATE 60) is plainer than any of those illustrated by Fowler, but sports octagonal columns for its porch as well as the octagonal chimney that appears in Fowler's designs. The material, however, is grout, not concrete (which was rarely employed in Ontario – or anywhere else, it seems – for such buildings). Possibly the most ambitious house of this type in Ontario is The Octagon in Port Hope (PLATE 59), which dates from 1856 and has a double veranda on six of its eight sides.

An isolated instance of the use of concrete also occurred in Port Hope at an early date – directly owing to the influence of

Fowler. The Port Hope *Weekly Guide* for 25 September, 1858 notes that 'Mr. David Smith is erecting a new house, of a material and in a manner almost entirely new in this section of the country. The walls are constructed upon stone foundations, of concrete, according to a method propagated, and by many supposed to have been invented, by those indefatigable water-cure and so-called Reform Publishers, the Messrs. Fowler of New York.' But the form was apparently not octagonal: 'The style of Mr. Smith's house . . . is an approach to Tudor or Elizabethan Gothic. Irregularity of horizontal outline, projecting Bays, Mullion'd and Transom'd windows, with a steeply pitched roof, Dormers and small gables form its character. Doubtless, when finished it will be highly picturesque.'

Shortly after the middle of the century, houses incorporating some elements of the Gothic Revival style became widespread in this province; the choice of this style tended to reinforce the popularity, or even dictate the adoption, of board and batten as a covering in preference to clapboard. The core of a rambling, hill-side house known as The Cone, in Port Hope (PLATE 51), can be related to the H.H. Boody house in Brunswick, Maine, of 1848-49 by Gervase Wheeler, which Downing had illustrated and discussed at length in *The Architecture of Country Houses*. Both are large houses which turn paired gables to the street and give an appearance of irregularity because of the complex roof patterns and the use of features like the bay window. Both are contructed of board and batten, that wide vertical boarding with joints covered by a narrow batten, which Downing liked for many reasons. He maintained that board and batten was more economical than clapboard and, 'being a bolder method of construction, it better expresses the picturesque beauty essentially belonging to wooden houses.' Above all, he favoured it 'not only because it is more durable, but because it has an expression of strength and truthfulness . . . . The main timbers which enter into the frame of a wooden house and support the structure, are vertical, and hence the vertical boarding properly signifies to the eye a wooden house.'[26]

Board and batten was commonly used in much smaller houses, like that in Elora (PLATE 56). Such houses, usually a storey and a half, and frequently carrying on the veranda tradition of the Ontario cottage, but now with a steeply-pitched gable or 'peak' centred over the door, were very often enriched with decorative bargeboards under the raking eaves—in Gothic Revival fashion.

In Canada such frame houses were apparently painted in colours compatible with their surroundings—presumably influenced again by Downing. He deplored the use of 'glaring,' 'dazzling' white because 'it does not harmonize with the country, and thereby mars the effect of rural landscapes . . . . It stands harshly apart from all the soft shades of the scene.' Instead, 'Earth, stone, bricks and wood, are the substances that enter mostly into the structure of our houses, and from these we would accordingly take suggestions.' He quoted Sir Joshua Reynold's remark that 'If you would fix upon the best color for your house, turn up a stone, or pluck up a handful of grass by the roots, and see what is the color of the soil where the house is to stand, and let that be your choice.' Downing went on: 'the feeling that prompted it was . . . the necessity of a unity of color in the house and the country about it . . . . The color of all buildings in the country, should be those *soft and quiet shades* called neutral tints, such as fawn, drab, gray, brown, etc.' Downing also advised that 'we . . . adapt the shade of color . . . to the expression, style, or character of the house itself. Thus, a large mansion may very properly receive a somewhat sober hue, expressive of dignity; while a country house of moderate size demands a lighter and more pleasant, but still quiet tone; and a small cottage should . . . always have a cheerful and lively tint . . . . A certain sprightliness is . . . always bestowed . . . by painting the bolder projecting features of a different shade.'[27] Canadians have enjoyed a reputation—whether deservedly or not—for being more retiring than their American neighbours; in any case, it used to be true where the colouring of their respective houses was concerned. Downing's admonitions seem to have had little effect in the United States, but not all Ontario houses were painted white and shutter green by any means. Many of the latter were much more 'racy of the soil.'

Few of these board and batten houses survive in anything like original condition. Most of them were later clad in a thin skin of brick or in the composition sheathing known as insulbrick. In the former case, the absence of headers—bricks turned endwise to bond two parallel courses of stretchers (bricks laid lengthwise)—may indicate the presence of a board and batten house underneath.

But many houses of the same basic pattern were built entirely of brick in the first instance; some with boldly-patterned facades reflected the new interest of the 1850s in Italian mediaeval brickwork. Ornamental bands of coloured brick are to be found under the eaves, while the quoins, window-heads and doorhead also received attention. Patterns were created both by stepping the bricks forward or back and by using different colours of brick. Typically, red and so-called white (yellow) bricks were used; occasionally black bricks were produced by dipping in tar or creosote.[28] The same devices could, of course, be applied to the older and simpler conventions of form, as in the fine Mennonite farmhouse of patterned brick near Stouff-

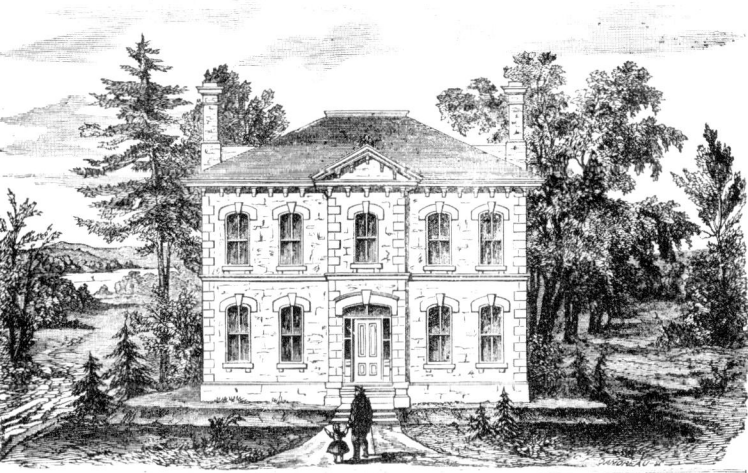

6

ville (PLATE 63). Later still, in row houses like those in Whitby (PLATE 91), patterned brick could also be used – with bay windows and glazed porches – to distinguish one unit from another in a terrace.

The only asymmetric plan widely used in this province featured a projecting wing across one end, with the entrance at the angle between the body of the house and the wing. Most American pattern books of the mid-century contained at least one such design, and a British prototype for all of these appears in that still earlier and very influential work, J.C. Loudon's *Encyclopaedia of Cottage, Farm, and Villa Architecture and Furniture* (London, 1833).[29] None of the examples was richer than that illustrated in the *Canada Farmer* in 1864 (fig. 6, lower). Plans and elevations of such model houses were published (at irregular intervals) in this periodical under the title 'Rural Architecture' or 'Farm Architecture.' In most instances, the designs were equally applicable to urban situations, and the subtitle appearing with this one actually refers to the design as a 'Suburban Villa or Farm House.' Typically, some sort of architectural association seemed to be required, and it was said that 'This design partakes of the early English character.' It could be 'built with either brick, wood or stone, without interfering with the design.' The house differed from earlier types in two respects. It formalized the increasingly common practice of providing paired and communicating parlours by grouping these in the wing, and it employed varied detailing – bay window, veranda, bargeboards and exposed wood trusses – to enhance this asymmetric and picturesque form.

Equally asymmetric are the Italianate or Tuscan villas like the Rectory at Niagara-on-the-Lake (PLATE 65), which dates from 1858. These are built on a rather similar plan, but with a tall, square tower that runs through the inner angle of the veranda or replaces it altogether; in either case, the tower forms the focus of the design.[30] Tuscan villas in North America are generally large houses with the loftier storeys characteristic of the latter half of the century, but such houses in Ontario are very much less ostentatiously detailed than British or American examples.

These villas are harbingers of a dramatic change in scale more often associated with the equally vertically-oriented but more lavishly ornamented mansions in 'French Renaissance' (or Second Empire) style. The house on Wellington Street South in Goderich (PLATE 88) is such a house, with its restless succession of wall planes, its elaborately-carved window jambs, and its iron-crested, patterned-slate roofs of complex form culminating in a curved mansard roof on the tall, octagonal corner tower.[31] The new visual scale – which resulted from much intricate detailing on an irregular profile of such tall dimensions—appeared in the third quarter of the century in all kinds of architecture, but it is more often found in public and commercial buildings than in private houses. Few families could have afforded such a pretentious structure as either the dignified Italianate villa or the bombastic French house; in fact, both Tuscan villa and Renaissance mansion are comparatively rare in Ontario towns.

The sedate farmhouse north of Waterford (PLATE 86) and the house on Queen Street in Kincardine (PLATE 87) may be taken as far more representative of the decades from the 1860s almost to the close of the century. These houses would still have been considered Italianate with their bracketed eaves and large, arched windows with round-headed lights—filled with the enormous panes of glass widely available in the 1870s. The farmhouse is especially strongly patterned, with its carefully-pieced fieldstone, its overwrought entrance and 'Tuscan Gothic' window above, and its turned and fretted brackets. But both houses conform to the description given by the *Canada Farmer* for a farmhouse—designed to order by the magazine for a correspondent—in 1865 (fig. 6, upper): 'The monotony of the front is relieved by projecting the hall two feet forward of the main building. This is carried up and finished with a gable.' 'The exterior is simply designed; there is no attempt to make it all corners and gables, it is simply a straightforward square house.'[32]

---

[1] For example, the Stoddard-Hayes house of 1822 in Lisle, N.Y., resembles the central portion of the Barnum house; see Eugene D. Montillon, *Historic Architecture in Broome County, New York and Vicinity* (Binghamton, 1972), p. 56. For British parallels, see the 'First-rate House' in [Peter Nicholson], *New Practical Builder, and Workman's Companion* (London, 1823-[25]), p. 563.

[2] Quoted in Arthur R. M. Lower, *Canadians in the Making: A Social History of Canada* (Toronto, 1958), p. 166.

[3] Exemplary for the way in which American buildings are related to British prototypes, relatively little-known in many cases, is the recent work by William H. Pierson, Jr., *American Buildings and Their Architects; The Colonial and Neoclassical Styles* (Garden City, [1970]).

[4] Isaac Ware, *A Complete Body of Architecture. Adorned with Plans and Elevations, from Original Designs* (London, 1756), p. 299.

[5] Quoted in Jeanne Minhinnick, *At Home in Upper Canada* (Toronto, 1970), p. 45; see also pp. 46, 59 regarding domestic help.

[6] Such work is handsomely illustrated in E. Graeme Robertson, *Early Buildings of Southern Tasmania* (2 vols.: Melbourne, 1970). Except for their detailing, many of these buildings are analogous to stone buildings in Ontario.

[7] Regarding the date of the Manor see Verschoyle Benson Blake and Ralph Greenhill, *Rural Ontario* [Toronto, 1969], pp. 16-17.

[8] John Ross Robertson, ed., *The Diary of Mrs. John Graves Simcoe* (Toronto, 1934), p. 110 re Kingston and p. 127 re the Hamilton house at Niagara. For a view of the first stone house in Kingston and a note on its subsequent history, see J. Douglas Stewart and Ian E. Wilson, *Heritage Kingston* (Kingston, [1973]), pp. 46-47.

[9] Blake and Greenhill, *Rural Ontario*, p. 19.
[10] William Bell, *Hints to Emigrants; in a Series of Letters from Upper Canada* (Edinburgh, 1824), pp. 223-24, and [Catherine Parr Traill], *The Backwoods of Canada: being Letters from the Wife of an Emigrant Officer, Illustrative of the Domestic Economy of British America* (London, 1836), pp. 93-97, contain good descriptions of shanties.
[11] *The Autobiography of John Galt* (2 vols: London, 1833), II. 59.
[12] *Journal of the Legislative Assembly of the Province of Canada*, 1857, Vol. IX Appendix 54.
[13] Such dummy windows were more common in the gables; unfortunately the Barnum gable window has not been painted to preserve the illusion. For a door which is comparable in design, see the severely simple frame house of 1780 in A.E. Richardson and H. Donaldson Eberlein, *The Smaller English House of the Later Renaissance*, 1660-1830 (New York, [1925]), fig. 94. The type was also common in the southern and middle American colonies in the third quarter of the eighteenth century; it was found in the north during the last quarter of that century and the early years of the next. Eliakim Barnum was, in fact, a Loyalist from Vermont.
[14] Australia was apparently the only other British colony where the elliptical fan over rectangular sidelights achieved comparable popularity, to judge from plates in J.M. Freeland, *Architecture in Australia: A History* (Melbourne, [1968]).
[15] Blake and Greenhill, *Rural Ontario*, pp. 24-25.
[16] Eric R. Arthur, *The Early Buildings of Ontario* ([Toronto], 1938), p. [15], suggests that the gable was used to throw snow away from the doorstep—which, experience suggests, is hardly a consideration. The fact is that a windowless upper hall in a storey-and-a-half house is very dark and solemn.
[17] See especially 'The Veranda and the Veranda House' in Ronald Lewcock, *Early Nineteenth Century Architecture in South Africa* (Cape Town, 1963), pp. 110-30. In Australia, too, 'the verandah was . . . to become the most important feature of Colonial architecture,' according to Freeland, *Architecture in Australia*, p. 47.
[18] In the work of A.J. Downing and his circle, the veranda rather contrarily takes a particularly elaborate form.
[19] The classic description of the piazza is in John Singleton Copley's letter to Henry Pelham in 1771; see [Sydney] Fiske Kimball, *Domestic Architecture of the American Colonies and of the Early Republic* (New York, 1966), pp. 98-99.
[20] Andrew Bell, 'Building Stones of Eastern Ontario,' *The Canadian Architect and Builder*, IX (March 1896). 42-43.
[21] Marion MacRae and Anthony Adamson, *The Ancestral Roof; Domestic Architecture of Upper Canada* (Toronto, 1963), p. [59].
[22] Howard is one nineteenth-century architect for whom a slender biographic sketch—an autobiography—exists: *Incidents in the Life of John G. Howard, Esq. of Colborne Lodge, High Park, near Toronto; Chiefly Adapted from His Journals* (Toronto, 1885). In the *Catalogue of Paintings in the Gallery at Colborne Lodge*, p. 15, bound with the foregoing, are noted 219 volumes that he gave the city; of these 34 are volumes of the *Builder*, an exceedingly important architectural journal published in London for the professional designer and those in the building trades, beginning in 1842. There would not appear to have been anything else of significance architecturally, to judge by the items listed here, or those in the 'List of Architectural Books in the Toronto Public Library,' *Canadian Architect and Builder*, I, no. VI (June 1888), 6-7: the one outstanding early nineteenth-century book of any potential use in Ontario which is listed in the latter notice is John Claudius Loudon's important and comprehensive work, *An Encyclopaedia of Cottage, Farm, and Villa Architecture and Furniture*, first published in London in 1833.
[23] Many of the books which Cumberland brought and those he subsequently bought are now in the University of Toronto Library system.
[24] The house design illustrated by Ruttan in plates VII-IX appears to be an Ontario building but is, in fact, only a Canadian modification of the Southern House in Gervase Wheeler, *Rural Homes; or Sketches of Houses Suited to American Country Life* (Auburn, 1853), facing p. 132 and p. 135. In addition to a plausibly Ontario church, plates XXVII-XXIX, Ruttan identifies one house, plate XXXIV, as 'Plan of small cottage . . . Designed and Drawn by

W. Graeme Tomkins Archt. St. Marys, C.W.'

[25] For bibliographic details on these and other works, see Henry-Russell Hitchcock, *American Architectural Books: A List of Books, Portfolios and Pamphlets on Architecture and Related Subjects Published in America before 1895* (Minneapolis, [1962]).

[26] A.J. Downing, *The Architecture of Country Houses* (New York, 1850), pp. 51-52. It may be noted here that although the use of board and batten was introduced in the United States in the late 1830s, and common by mid-century, its use in Ontario may have been delayed: the text accompanying 'Rural Architecture: A Cheap Farm House,' *Canada Farmer*, I (15 November, 1864). 340, suggests that clapboarding was still more common, at that late date, than board and batten.

[27] Downing, *The Architecture of Country Houses*, pp. 201-04. Less specifically, Canadians were advised that 'The exterior of the building should be painted some nice fawn or light buff colour': 'Architecture. Design of a Small Farm Dwelling,' *Canada Farmer*, New Series, III (16 January, 1871). 17.

[28] John Ruskin made a few references to brick in his widely-read work, *The Stones of Venice* (London, 1851-53), but the really influential book was written by George Edmund Street, *Brick and Marble in the Middle Ages: Notes of a Tour in the North of Italy* (London, 1855). The latter work went into a second edition as late as 1874 and contained detailed chromolithographs of patterned (and moulded) brick designs.

[29] Loudon, *Encyclopaedia*, p. 226, Design LXXV.

[30] In principle, this one is close to Design VI for 'An irregular villa in the Italian Style' illustrated in Downing, *Cottage Residences*, although Downing's design is a mirror image and in frame.

[31] *Godey's Magazine* (or *Godey's Lady's Book*), the most widely read magazine in nineteenth-century North America, reproduced many houses characterized by the same features (and collectively dubbed Mansard Madness by a critical architect), especially in the 1870s. One of these, by Isaac H. Hobbs and Son, for a much larger house, illustrated *ibid*., XC (April 1875), may well have influenced the design of that in Goderich. On the 'Lady's Book houses,' see George L. Hersey, 'Godey's Choice,' *Journal of the Society of Architectural Historians*, XVIII (1959). 104-11.

[32] 'Rural Architecture: A Two-Story Farm House,' *Canada Farmer*, II (15 April, 1865). 116. Earlier, *ibid*., II (1 March, 1865). 72, the editors noted that 'A correspondent requests us to furnish the plan of a two-story stone farmhouse, 28×42. We shall be happy to do so, if the party ... will inform us what kind of accommodation is required, number and description of rooms, &c. It would be well to state the size of the family ... whether quarters are needed for a hired man, or for a domestic servant, together with any other details that will help to make it suit the purpose of the owner and occupants.' The editor obliged with the design reproduced here, which followed six weeks later.

MEETING HOUSES & CHURCHES

Church architecture in Ontario is astonishingly varied, more so than domestic architecture. The main reason for this was the 'amazing diversity of sects in Upper Canada,' remarked upon by Sir Richard Bonnycastle in *The Canadas in* 1841. In addition to the nicely balanced numbers of Anglicans, Presbyterians and Catholics, Sir Richard observed that 'the most respectable and numerous [sects] are the Primitive Methodists, Baptists, Unitarians, Independents, or Congregationalists, and Quakers.'

This diversity had important architectural consequences in the numbers both of individual structures and of different types of structures. The typical New England town was dominated by one church, but many vied for prominence in the Ontario town. Commonly, each of these could be formally distinguished from its neighbours, as the various denominations had different traditions of architecture as well as of worship. Though churches were generally rectangular in plan, with the height roughly half the length, the treatment of the walls was varied. This was not just an exercise in the design of facades; the fabric embodied the intensely-felt religious principles of the denomination, to a degree not always intended.

Two churches in the eastern portion of the province illustrate this well, though built only a few years apart. The Methodist White Chapel north of Picton (PLATE 4), begun in 1809 and apparently completed two years later, is very much like New England meeting houses of the seventeenth century—a frame building, nearly cubic, under a hipped roof which is nearly pyramidal.[1] Its purity and precision of form amount to a moral precept. By contrast, St. Andrew's Presbyterian Church in Williamstown (PLATE 27), begun in 1812 and completed in 1818, was distinctly ambitious and even elegant, though not advanced by the standards of the early nineteenth century. Its windows anticipated the repeated use of the Palladian motif at Riverest in L'Orignal (PLATE 28). At St. Andrew's, each window opening contains a fully developed classical order in the vertical mullions (complete with horizontal architrave), and the whole is enclosed by a round-headed arch in unique fashion. The result is a memorial to the prosperity granted God's Presbyterian elect and an earnest of their devotion.

Three other structures, built for as many denominations and scattered across the southern centre of the province, point up instead the remarkable serviceability of the simple rectangular building with a low-pitched gable roof.

The earliest is the Anglican Church of St. Mary Magdalene,

Picton (PLATE 23), a brick building which has been much altered. Erected in 1825-27, it was later lengthened at either end and given a new, massive, thick-walled tower. Its ecclesiastical function was suggested by the pointed windows with intersecting glazing bars in the double-hung sash – the so-called switchline tracery more popular in small contemporary Irish churches than in English examples. At this early date in Upper Canada, probably only the Anglicans would have approved and valued the association implicit in the use of such windows: that Pointed or Gothic style was to be identified with Christian architecture.[2]

Apart from its graveyard, the Mennonite Church of 1853 at Altona (PLATE 37) is less obviously a place of worship. It follows the pattern of plain meeting houses associated with the Society of Friends in Ontario. The Canadian Friends affirmed 'plainness of speech, behaviour and apparel' monthly at their services and simplicity carried over naturally into their meeting houses. These almost always had two doors, commonly in the long face between symmetrically-arranged windows; one door was used by the men, the other by the women. At Altona, however, the second door gives access to a vestibule running across the end of the structure.

By virtue of a change in the scale of the door and windows (though little change in the size of the building) and a shift in the axis, the religious function is made more explicit in the Bethel Chapel, near Kilbride (PLATE 38). In this remarkable work of 1853, the entrance is moved to the gable end, the customary position in most of the religious architecture of Ontario. Both the door and windows attain a scale that indicates its public character. In fact, in Ontario such a monumental door would be found only in a church.

The simple rectangular building could be readily expanded or reduced, and at one time the smaller end of the scale was represented by numerous log churches. Few survive, though Providence Church, c.1845, from Kitley Township in Leeds County and now in Upper Canada Village, is probably representative.

For the more ambitious congregation in the early years of the province, an alternative was to make use of a pattern book, modifying the plates as desired, and this was done in 1831 at one of the most famous churches in the province, St. Andrew's Presbyterian at Niagara-on-the-Lake (PLATE 14). Although a Scottish kirk, it was adapted from *The American Builder's Companion* by Asher Benjamin. Few early pattern books reproduced appropriate designs for churches, but Benjamin's book – which had been published as early as 1806 – had recently (1827) gone into its sixth edition, with the addition of several church plans.

One of these was followed closely at St. Andrew's (fig. 7).

Comparison of St. Andrew's with Benjamin's designs and with the original contract drawings for the church points up a number of interesting changes, however.[3] First, the irregularly spaced and rather delicately proportioned Roman Doric columns of Benjamin's design were changed to follow what the original specifications call 'Cooper's Plan, the Grecian Doric.' Cooper must have drafted the original designs, and is presumably James Cooper, a member of the congregation. He must have had an eye to advancing fashion in suggesting regularly spaced Doric columns of particularly massive proportions, carrying an exceedingly heavy architrave in the Greek Revival mode. These were scaled down somewhat in execution, but the extra expense of these stout orders was more than offset by omitting the responding pilasters against the front wall of the church. The flanks were intended to be panelled with blind arcades framing the windows, as in Benjamin's design (and the nearby brick house on Queen Street, [PLATE 12]). This feature was omitted and a compromise was also effected between Benjamin's three round-headed doors and Cooper's three square-headed. The dependence on Benjamin extends to the windows, which are enriched externally to follow – curiously enough – his internal elevations, omitting the jambs and panels. Together with Cooper's quoined corners, the result is less crisp than Benjamin's design, and much less stringent than American Greek Revival work. Cooper's tower, which had a square stage followed by three octagonal stages having Doric colonnettes at the angles of their upper and lower storeys and an octagonal spire, was redesigned. Borrowing a square stage from another of Benjamin's designs (for a meeting house), combining it with the first octagonal stage of the design for a church which is reproduced here, and topping it off with a simple octagonal spire produced the spectacularly abrupt sequence of forms seen today.

If St. Andrew's Presbyterian is tentative but effective Greek Revival design, the Anglican Church of the Holy Trinity at Chippawa (PLATE 26) is a Gothic Revival work of comparable quality and equally distinctive. It was designed by John Howard in July 1840 to replace a building burnt in 1839, and was completed in 1841.[4] The oblong block with a square tower breaking the centre of the west front is basically mediaeval in plan, a form which never passed out of use in England, and recurred increasingly from the mid-eighteenth century on. But a chancel was a more variable element, and was here omitted; as a result of this and because the tower projects into the body of the church, Holy Trinity appears to be nearly square inside. Plainly finished, the interior almost resembles that of a meeting house.

In Howard's church the Gothic vocabulary is used with the cheerful self-consciousness of late Georgian architecture. Howard delighted in each newly-learned word or phrase, so to speak, and quoted these elements out of context. He applied Gothic and Classical details indiscriminately to what was, once again, a simple rectangular structure. Arched openings, traceried windows (subsequently altered), pinnacles at the corners of the tower, and a spiky spire on top of the tall belfry stage — all those gothicizing details are vertically oriented; even the battlements give the church height, in an attempt to disguise a basically horizontal mass.

The design is a blunt mixture, boldly patterned. The openings in the masonry are all classically keyed (alternately long and short), nowhere more beautifully than around the almond-shaped window (a gothicizing motif). Other basically Classical elements, like the quoins at the corners of the building and the little rectangular dentils under the eaves, marry up with the big-toothed battlements. The combination of brick and stone is dramatic, but the transition to white-painted wood is harsh, especially in the area of the battlemented parapet. Even though this is aligned with the principal facade, it sits on the projecting cornice as a sort of boomtown Gothic; it is really a false front applied to a gabled roof to create an ecclesiastical billboard which will announce what 'A mighty fortress is our God.' From this point on, the Gothic revival would assume a position of prominence in Upper Canada.

Against this background, an Italianate church like the Presbyterian one at Colborne (PLATE 20) is exceptional in Ontario. The church is dated 1830 on the face of the tower; an inscription found under the pulpit stated that it was 'projected by Archibald Fraser builder and undertaker [contractor].' it has an entrance tower engaged in the end wall, and is Italianate, or Tuscan, to the extent that it has deeply-projecting eaves carried on paired brackets and a flat profile to the roof of the tower, which is of compressed rectangular plan. The windows have all been filled with stained glass at a later date, altering the effect of the church internally as well as externally. (The rather later Methodist Church at Actinolite [PLATE 46], built in 1864-66 to the design of a Belleville architect, A.J. Stapely, illustrates a particularly elaborate example of the Tuscan window.) The belfry stage of the tower at Colborne has clean-cut, round-arched openings which create dark shadows within the otherwise unaccented stone mass; such umbrage was also associated with the Tuscan mode. This belfry is, however, a remarkably sympathetic replacement of 1910.

8

In another sense, however, the Colborne church is characteristic of early Ontario. As characteristic as St. Andrew's, St. Mary Magdalene or, for that matter, the White Chapel. All of these are plain to the point of austerity. Strong in profile, from any distance they appear smooth in surface and positive in mass. The openings are equally affirmative in character; relatively small in proportion to the total wall, these voids appear to have been punched neatly out of the planes that so clearly enclose the space within.

St. John's Roman Catholic Church in Perth (PLATE 32), built in 1848, represents the most knowing, and also the most telling, use of this plain Ontario style. It stands on Wilson Street at Brock, a residential street which it completely commands. Such siting is peculiarly Irish, more characteristic of the Established Church than the Roman Catholic, though—following the long-delayed Emancipation Act of 1829—the Catholics finally began to express their release in dramatically-sited and stunningly-scaled churches. There were concentrations of Irish throughout the area and these were years of intense immigration from Ireland. The church was built for a priest with an Irish name, Father John H. McDonough, and the builders themselves may well have been Irish. Certainly there is a strong general resemblance to highly original work of the 1820s by a Dublin architect, John Semple, who created what is aptly called spike Gothic in Irish churches like that at Kilternan (fig. 8). Semple's churches are of much cruder surface than is customary in other parts of the United Kingdom, and very strikingly massed, with tall clusters made up of a tower that is narrower than usual and corner turrets that are nearly as large. Simple openings of comparably exaggerated proportions are used to create ambivalent scale relationships. But at Perth the repeated mouldings which give verve to Semple's work are lacking. The absence of these lends the Perth church, even more than the Irish ones, the appearance of a large toy.

Christ Church, Lakefield (PLATE 47), of 1853-54, is also a product of the Gothic Revival, but singularly advanced for this province, even by Anglican standards. Its highly picturesque character and sophisticated execution are representative of mid-century trends and serve to distinguish it from all earlier churches. But Lakefield had literary settlers: Colonel Samuel Strickland and his sisters, Mrs. Catherine Parr Traill and Mrs. Susanna Moodie. The architect of Christ Church was Strickland's son-in-law, Kivas Tully.

Kivas Tully (1820-1905) was born in southern Ireland and came to Toronto in 1844, bringing fresh ideas with him.[5] He was in the vanguard of a remarkable influx of talent that continued to emigrate from the United Kingdom through the

1850s. These two decades, the 1840s and 1850s, were years of enormous consequence in terms of artistic theory, technological developments and architectural practice. Compared with Howard's Holy Trinity, Tully's Christ Church, Lakefield, is the work of a 'true goth' of the mid-century with a full command of both the vocabulary and syntax of mediaeval design.

By the 1840s, the Ecclesiological Society had made its influence felt throughout the English-speaking world. The Society was an English organization of Anglican clergy, churchmen, architects and architectural amateurs, all with leanings toward the High Church. In principle they maintained that doctrinally the reformed church differed little from the pre-Reformation church and, accordingly, the mediaeval structures which had served the English Church so well were still appropriate. In their view, Gothic form was also necessary in new construction if the ancient services were to be conducted in a meaningful manner. Further, they were devoted to the proposition that in order to learn how to advance in the future, it was necessary to return for a period to a close examination, or even imitation, of the patterns of the past. Highly susceptible to the theory of the Picturesque, they firmly believed that constituents like variety, irregularity and roughness of form — what Ruskin called changefulness and savageness or rudeness — were essential manifestations of the rational and functional bases of mediaeval design.[6] Above all, they were reformers who aimed at an artistic revolution which would revitalize religious values and effect in turn a social transformation.

In accordance with such aims, Tully adopted at Lakefield what is sometimes called the neo-mediaeval plan. The massing of the church is complex, even though the building is small. For each different function, a structurally discrete space is provided. The main body of the church is compact and low. A narrower, lower chancel holds the Holy Table and extends the long axis. A still smaller porch (considered to be appropriately expressive of humility) juts asymmetrically to one side. The church has no pretentious tower — it is a chapel and content with a bell in a gabled bellcote at the ridge. The only ornament consists of frankly structural elements like the large diagonal buttresses at each angle of the building. Everything is very earnest and, in the contemporary phrase, essentially real.

Relatively few architects have been identified with individual buildings in the towns and villages of Ontario, and Kivas Tully is a special case — he is probably the only architect of note whose work may be regarded as both a strong feature in the townscape and yet an integral part of it. We have already seen his design for a house in Weston which is within the Ontario tradition. Remarkably, he could also design a structure like Christ Church which represented the advanced taste of the Anglican High Church by its convincing air of antiquity. Yet Christ Church has a sense, simultaneously, of fully belonging to the place and expressing its spirit. The *genius loci*, as the Victorians liked to call that quality, is conveyed through the design, which in spite of its picturesque properties is still a no-nonsense, heavily-proportioned one, and through the equally blunt, workmanlike handling of the coursed rubble masonry. The result may therefore be compared with those earlier churches of frame, brick and stone already cited as buildings which not only happen to be located in this province but are also quintessentially of it.

Even if such high ideals were imperfectly appreciated by others, resistance to the Gothic forms collapsed and they were carried over into wood, a material foreign to the style. Accordingly, the Presbyterians adapted the full range of a Gothic mason's vocabulary to 'carpenter's Gothic' in wood at St. Andrew's Church in Maple, in 1862 (PLATE 53). It used to be fashionable to excoriate such builders for their clapboard walls, plank buttresses and wooden tracery. But they were delighted by the rich formal possibilities of Gothic Revival style, aware of the varieties of meaning it could bear, and conscious of the responsive material in which they worked. They transformed the structure, elements and proportions accordingly.

At a more ambitious level, High Victorian Gothic of the 1860s and 1870s is most interesting for the distinctive sense of form which reaches maturity in these years, and the experiments with materials to exploit their textural, colouristic, or structural possibilities. The two go hand in hand in an Anglican church like All Saints', Whitby, designed in 1864 and built in 1865-66, and its school house (PLATE 80). The first is by Gundry and Langley; the second, designed in 1870, is by Henry Langley working on his own.

The use of brick in church-building was rarely approved by High Churchmen before the late 1840s, except for churches considered to be temporary, because the material was regarded as inferior to stone; thereafter it came to be valued because it lent continuity to a church erected among other brick buildings, and also for its peculiar properties. Clearly, Langley enjoyed brick and the opportunity to erect smooth planes of great extent with sharp profiles.

The profile of such Anglican churches in the 1860s is big-boned, self-confident, even aggressive. All Saints' is characteristic with its lofty, broad-spreading nave, one generous volume of space under a single roof. The latter is nicely contrasted with the dissonantly diverging roof planes of the low sacristy (next to the chancel) and the dramatically tall steeple on the corner tower.

Langley also enjoyed the possibility of employing more than one colour of brick to create energetic patterns that would cling to one planar surface. The church is basically red brick, but the windows—jambs, heads and tracery—are of yellow brick. In the schoolhouse Langley used the same two colours alternately in the window heads while banding the whole building with courses of yellow brick at sill level and near the window heads. Even the roofs were once colourfully patterned, the spire being 'covered with slate, ornamented in bands of various tints, the ribs ... covered with galvanized iron, surmounted with a wrought-iron finial, coloured in blue-and-gold.'[7]

High Victorian style was unusually non-sectarian in Ontario, as Langley's career demonstrates. Elsewhere in the English-speaking world it tended to be the preserve, where church architecture was concerned, of the Anglican Communion, and of the High Church, often in association with high society. But this was by no means always the case here. Architects were in short supply and their clientele crossed social and sectarian lines—more often than one might expect in Orange Ontario with all its peculiar ethnic patterns. Henry Langley (1836-1906) had an extremely wide range within his extensive, largely ecclesiastical, Toronto-based practice. In Oshawa alone he designed the Anglican Church, the Baptist Chapel and the Wesleyan Methodist Church. He was especially favoured by the Methodists and built Metropolitan Wesleyan Methodist Church (now Metropolitan United), the 'Cathedral of Methodism,' in Toronto. Elsewhere he did work for the Presbyterians, Primitive Methodists and Roman Catholics. Because so much of Ontario's church architecture stemmed from Langley's firm or reflected his influence, it tended to confer another kind of homogeneity on the Ontario townscape.

The design of 1874 reproduced here (fig. 9) is for a large masonry Wesleyan Methodist Church by Langley, Langley and Burke in Aylmer—on the Quebec side of the Ottawa River—and illustrates a variation on the Anglican type which was tremendously popular with Ontario Protestants, particularly Methodists and Presbyterians. Superficially it strongly resembles a church like All Saints', Whitby. But the low polygonal form, which at first glance looks like a chancel, proves to be a church school with lecture room at the ground level—connecting with the church proper—and Sunday School rooms above. Typically, such churches are elevated well above ground level, partly to provide an auditorium at the lower level; in such cases the Sunday School wing might be omitted. Consequently, they are almost always equipped with an en-

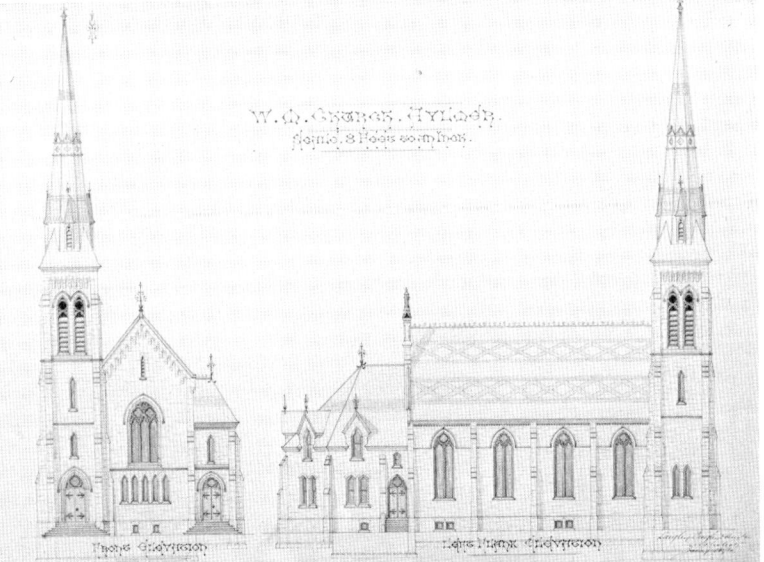

trance—often paired, as here—above impressive steps, leading to a lobby with stairs to a gallery. A gallery was now considered unthinkable by most Anglicans, who felt it lent a theatrical air to a church; if present, it was confined to the rear portion of their churches. In this church, as many Methodist and Presbyterian churches, the gallery extends around all four sides, acting as choir and organ loft behind a centrally located pulpit on a raised platform.

A building method generally associated with the Anglicans and used by others in churches of this sort from the 1870s is seen in the United Church in Whitevale (PLATE 82); brick laid in various positions so as to break the plane strikingly. In the method known as corbelling, each successive course of brick is laid farther forward, overhanging the previous one, to create the connected series of bracketed forms—a corbel table—closing off the top of the wall with a jagged shadow line. In another method, imbrication, the bricks are laid at roughly 45 degrees to the wall plane to create a tough, knuckle-like series of projections, usually around windows and doors. Both are used in Whitevale with considerable feeling and real power.

It is, finally, the board and batten churches like St. Thomas', Brooklin (PLATE 54), that represent an indigenous response in our church architecture. Despite the proximity of Brooklin to Toronto, St. Thomas' is the image of 'the true North,' 'the Hyperborean zone.' It is an image evoked equally in eastern Canada and the north-eastern United States (especially in New Brunswick and Maine), in this period. St. Thomas' dates from 1870 and is conventionally massed with separate porch, nave and chancel. But it represents a response —given of the Victorian preoccupation with technological and cultural progress, and the concern of High Victorian Gothicism for rational principles—to the peculiarly North American problem of architecture in wood. Wood was no longer considered a poor material after the middle of the century; it was argued instead that 'the material for a church should be that most abundant in the neighborhood of the proposed work,' for 'When the Creator has provided a vast store of material, it seems to be pointed out as the one to be employed.'[8] And the form taken here, as in much domestic work in the same period, was board and batten, employed for its compatible verticality and its structural expression. Both qualities are developed to an extreme here in the remarkably-framed belfry carried up the west end of the church. Equally rational is the treatment of the windows, which have angular heads and tracery made of straight members, to which wood lends itself more readily than the curved forms of arched openings and intersecting mullions. In short, the apparent simplicity and plainness of St. Thomas' is as disarming and elemental as those qualities in the earlier Ontario churches. This is both appealing and misleading, for what actually emerges is the most intellectual and deliberate architecture of its time in this province.

[1] The sole surviving seventeenth-century meeting house in New England is the well-known Old Ship Meeting House at Hingham, Mass., of 1681; the standard study of the development of this independent American type is Marian Card Donnelly, *The New England Meeting Houses of the Seventeenth Century* (Middletown, [1968]).

[2] It was A.W. Pugin who crystallized the viewpoint with polemical brilliance in *The True Principles of Pointed or Christian Architecture* (London, 1841), but the vaguer idea of associating Gothic style with church architecture had already gained currency.

[3] The drawings, signed by the contractors (John Edward Clyde and Saxton Burr), are reproduced in E.R. Arthur, *St. Andrew's Church, Niagara-on-the-Lake*, Bulletin 153 of the School of Engineering Research, University of Toronto (Toronto, 1938), pp. 7, 8. Unfortunately, these drawings have disappeared from sight.

[4] See Houses, note 22. His 'Journals' or 'Time Books' are deposited together with many of his drawings in the Baldwin Room of the Metropolitan Toronto Central Library (with the exception of the office journal for 1849-55, which is in the Ontario Archives).

[5] For a biographical notice with a list of work, see 'Mr. Kivas Tully,' *The Canadian Architect and Builder*, XVIII (May 1905). 68.

[6] The influential essay on 'The Nature of Gothic' in John Ruskin, *The Stones of Venice*, II (London, 1853) did not appear until after the Ecclesiologists were confirmed in their love of picturesque form, but came to similar conclusions in more colourful and memorable language.

[7] Elsewhere two kinds of stone were used with the same effect to produce varied colouration of a lasting nature, dubbed 'permanent polychromy,' as in the Methodist Church, Harrowsmith (PLATE 81). Drawings for Whitby church and schoolhouse survive in the Langley Group collection in the Ontario Archives. (Other drawings are in the Metropolitan Toronto Central Library.) A booklet entitled *A Century of Worship*, published in 1966, reproduces most of the contemporary sources for the history of the church, including the description of the spire (from the *Whitby Chronicle* of 15 September, 1870).

[8] Charles Congdon, 'Wooden Churches,' *The New-York Ecclesiologist*, III (November 1851). 181, 185. For a discussion of the problem of a suitable church architecture in wood for North America, see Douglas Scott Richardson, 'Hyperborean gothic; or, wilderness Ecclesiology and the wood Churches of Edward Medley,' *Architectura*, [II], No. 1 (1972). 48-74.

PUBLIC BUILDINGS & SCHOOLS

10

An Act for Building a Gaol and Court-House in Every District—the first public buildings in the province—was passed as early as 1792. Lieutenant Governor Simcoe had originally subdivided Upper Canada into nineteen counties and grouped these into four districts for the administration of justice. In 1816 the Ottawa District was formed of Prescott and Russell Counties, and its Court House was erected at L'Orignal in 1824-25 by the contractors Donald McDonald and Walter Beckwith. This, the earliest surviving court house in Ontario, was a simple two-storey building of brown stone, five bays long, resembling a house. Wings added in 1861-62, a stiff, centrally-placed cupola, and other modifications have considerably lessened this resemblance. Like most court houses in Ontario, however, the structure turns its long face to the road and possesses a dramatic site—in this instance looking down a central street to the Ottawa River.

A court house of obviously public character was proposed in 1828 for Cobourg, then called Amherst, the seat of the Newcastle District. James Chewett (1793-1862), son of the first Deputy Surveyor-General of Upper Canada, submitted plans (now in the Ontario Archives) for this building, two sheets of which are reproduced here (fig. 10). Cells and jailer's apartments were provided in the vaulted basement. On the principal floor, a hall lay behind the central third of the front and an imposing courtroom beyond it, extending up through the second floor and even into the attic space. Rooms for the judges, lawyers, juries, witnesses and police surrounded the courtroom on the lower level, and 'Debtors Rooms' encircled it at the upper level. The plan was sensible, yet dignified.

The Court House elevation was ambitious. Centred on a porch, its pediment carried on a colossal, carefully-modelled Ionic order, the whole front was articulated by matching pilasters.

Yet Chewett would have had little experience on which to draw. He must have been the first native-born and fully professional architect in this province. At first glance one might think he had taken as his model one of the most impressive public buildings in the United Kingdom, the County Court House in York of 1765-77, but simplified and reduced it. He could have known the York building through George Richardson's *The New Vitruvius Britannicus* (London, 1808-10), one of the major publications of architectural designs in the early nineteenth century. But several small items in the detailing suggest that

Chewett drew on a still earlier prototype—a country house of the 1720s: his building is raised off the ground on a rusticated base, the columns are unevenly spaced, and the stairs sweep down at the sides in quarter-circles, all indications of an old-fashioned Palladianism rather than the current Neo-Classicism.

For some reason the design was redrafted by another architect before being put into construction. Chewett's design was dated 2 September, 1828, but in April 1829, Archibald Fraser signed another proposal (also in the Ontario Archives), which was accepted. Externally it hardly differed from Chewett's design: principally in increasing the height of the upper storey, but also in omitting the Royal coat of arms, and in rendering a somewhat naive treatment of the order, all of which weakened the design and made its scale ambiguous, especially about the entrance. Internally, Fraser's court house was much less formally laid out and the courtroom was a one-storey space restricted to the central portion of the upper level, as in most court houses built subsequently. According to the Quarter Sessions minutes, the Court House built on this plan was accepted in 1829 for an estimated cost of £4995 (plus £300 if the masonry were hammer-dressed or £580 if it were built of cut stone), and the building was in use, though not quite completed, in 1831. It had an extraordinarily short life-span: it lasted only a quarter of a century and was replaced in 1856 by Victoria Hall, which will be discussed later.

The Court House in Cobourg had hardly been completed when the Prince Edward County Court House was begun at Picton (PLATE 22) in 1832, again on the model of a house, this time of late Georgian character. According to the Hallowell *Free Press*, 14 February, 1832, the Justices of the Peace were to meet at Hopkins' Inn in Hallowell (which formed a large part of Picton) 'for the purpose of procuring and drawing up a plan and elevation of a Gaol and Court House to be built at Picton,' while another item, 13 March, 1832, noted that tenders were being called, still another, 7 April, 1834, that the unfinished-courtroom had been visted. Built of carefully-dressed masonry, it is essentially a two-storey Ontario house like the Alpheus Jones house in Prescott (PLATE 16), but considerably englarged. The colossal portico is still unevenly spaced but now of Greek Revival proportions and sitting at ground level. Together with the cupola it suggests a public function for the building, though the way in which the portico meets the court house and the form of the cupola both suggest that they were later additions.

The Districts were abolished by the Municipal Act of 1849, and the counties assumed their present judicial function; of all the court houses which followed in the early and middle 1850s, the Halton County Court House in Milton (fig. 11) is among

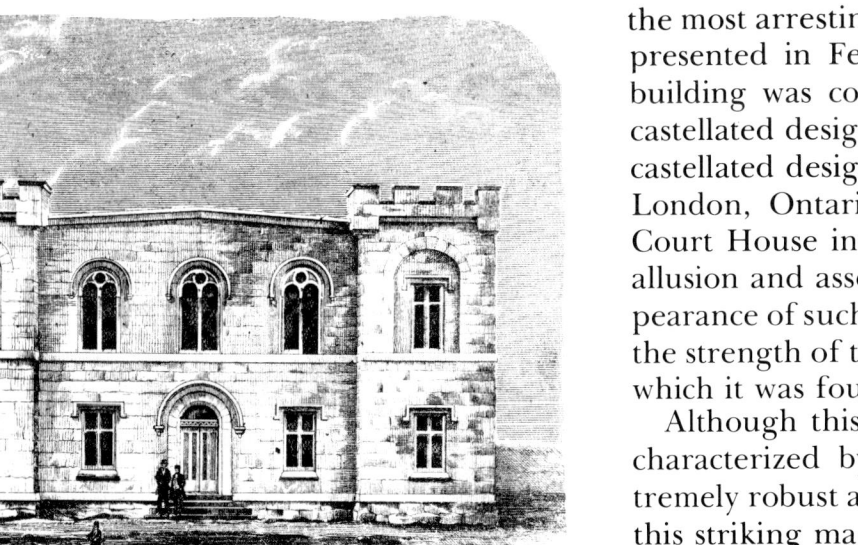

the most arresting. According to the town minutes, plans were presented in February 1854 by Clark and Murray and the building was considered complete in September 1855. The castellated design is apparently unique to Ontario. Two other castellated designs are the Middlesex County Court House in London, Ontario, of 1827-29, and the Wellington County Court House in Guelph, begun in 1841. In an age in which allusion and association were greatly valued, the fortified appearance of such designs was undoubtedly intended to suggest the strength of the law and the endurance of the principles on which it was founded.

Although this is, broadly, a symmetrical building and one characterized by very mixed detailing, the handling is extremely robust and lively. In the first place, the forcefulness of this striking mass is enhanced by the broad public square on which it fronts. Individual elements contribute to a sense of presence: except for the mouldings, the stone is in massive, rough-faced blocks, from the markedly sloping base to the overhanging battlements on the turrets. The irregularity is complemented by the fact that four lower windows are of the transomed 'Tudor Gothic' variety, while three upper windows in the centre are 'Tuscan Gothic.' These echo the round-headed doorway with its immense jambs, deeply angled like Romanesque work, and some Romanesque detailing is present: the chevrons between the transom light and the entrance door, and the varied corbels stopping the ends of all the mouldings above the arched windows. In the turrets, square-headed windows are set within shallow, round-headed panels – a happy compromise visually, if a curious one stylistically, to pull the elements together.

The Municipal Act of 1849, which had reframed the judicial districts, incorporated fifteen towns, including Brantford, Bytown, Cornwall, Dundas and London, which already had this status. The new towns were Belleville, Brockville, Cobourg, Goderich, Niagara, Peterborough, Picton, Port Hope, Prescott and St. Catharines. York, which became the city of Toronto in 1834, was joined by the new cities of Hamilton and Kingston. All the towns incorporated prior to the Act are cities today, with the one exception of Dundas. Its town hall (PLATE 44), built 1848-49, was the accomplished design of its local builder, Francis Hawkins.

The detailing of the Dundas town hall is highly individual, but the strong impact of the whole is typical of the town halls, which were generally broad, two-storey structures with a centrepiece topped by a central clock tower. It is a rectangle of carefully-dressed stone, but fitted to a triangle of land adjacent to the major approach to the town. Colossal pilasters are frequently used in town halls to link the levels and clasp the corners, while a small pediment is a common central accent. Here, a string-course breaks over the succession of pilasters in a decidedly unclassical way, and the centre is stessed by paired piers while the wall plane between remains deeply recessed. Typically a public hall was provided in the upper storey and the upper windows are round-arched at a larger scale as here. The cupola, which is octagonal in this case, has polygonal columns and provides space for a town clock.

Though contemporary sources often mention the orders employed in these buildings, there was clearly no intention to imitate the Classical tradition. Rather, they used forms freely to evoke an appearance of stability. The same sort of design, with numerous refinements, was employed by an American architect, Mervin Austin of Rochester, at Port Hope for the somewhat larger and more finished brick Town Hall of 1851 (visible at the right side of fig. 23).

Perth was not incorporated as a town until 1 January, 1854; its town hall (PLATE 73), dated 1863, illustrates the trend toward an Italianate treatment, a trend which became more marked after 1860, and the general development of an exaggerated verticality—both traits already noted in domestic architecture. Perth's Town Hall is typical of much Italianate work in Ontario in using the roughly but uniformly dressed ashlar stonework of the Scottish country mason and contrasting this nicely with rusticated blocks in the quoins and window jambs, and especially in the heavily-mannered pilasters of the doorcase. The triad of round-headed windows just above the entrance is a cliché of Ontario public buildings is the third quarter of the century. Every feature on the vertical axis at the centre is on the new large scale, and to fully appreciate this, one may contrast the fatness of the tower alone with the comparable portion in Asher Benjamin's church design half a century earlier (fig 7). But it is appropriate that a public building like the town hall should assert itself at this scale, and that the two-storey body of the building should rise to the same height as the neighbouring commercial structures of three storeys.

This new urban scale was already present and most superbly expressed in the old Huron District Court House in Goderich (fig. 12), completed in 1856. There the largeness of scale, complemented by richly-textured detailing, was both needed and effective, for the Court House stood in the middle of the great public square, a focus for the eight axes which radiated from it in the town's unique plan (fig. 13). Two identical fronts faced down East and West Streets: one toward the Huron Road which linked the town with the rest of the province; the other toward

12

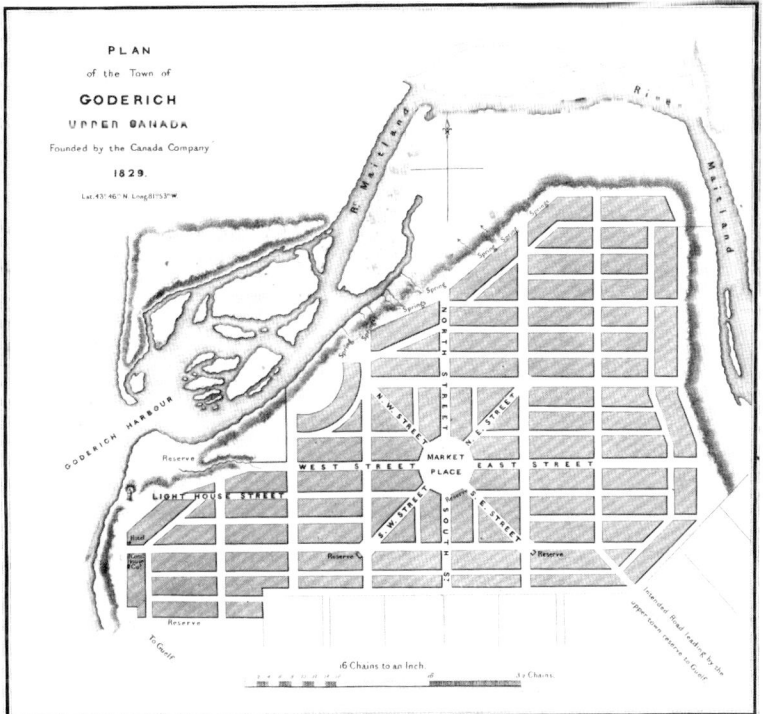

13

Lake Huron and the harbour which brought Goderich to prominence. Lesser fronts, almost miniatures of the principal facades, served as wings and commanded the vistas up North and South Streets. Even then, the so-called Square still seemed open and was accordingly planted with maples in 1871 or shortly before.[1] But despite the large scale, the whole complex had a humanizing rather than a brutalizing effect in that it controlled both the vast central space and the wide major arteries in this grandly-conceived town. The destruction of the Court House by fire in 1954 was tragic.

The fine adjustments of scale that characterize nineteenth-century public architecture in Ontario are demonstrated equally in Victoria Hall, Cobourg (PLATE 66). This remarkable multiple-use building was erected in 1856-60 to the design of Kivas Tully, the architect of Christ Church, Lakefield, who had also designed St. Peter's Church, Cobourg, in 1850. Victoria Hall was to serve as court house, town hall, assembly room, and masonic hall. The complex structure is modelled to some extent on Toronto's St. Lawrence Hall, but with a double portico like those on Osgoode Hall in Toronto. Victoria Hall is set back slightly from the street to give greater breadth to the principal thoroughfare, a better comprehension of the building as a whole, and a sense of its interaction with neighbouring structures. Although it appears colossal when viewed in isolation or through photographs, the size of individual components like the arcade in the portico is almost diminutive: what might be taken at first sight for a civic monument of ambitious force and overweaning scale proves instead to be fitted perfectly to the nature of the community, demonstrating Tully's remarkable finesse once again.

A common adjunct of the town hall was a market hall, often applied to the rear of the building, as at Perth, while a jail was frequently built within its own wall in proximity to the rear of the court house, as at Napanee.

The jail at Goderich, however, was quite separate, and preceded the Court House. The Huron District covered a large area—the counties of Bruce, Huron and Perth—and the jail built to serve it is one of the most distinguished buildings in the province (PLATE 21). It was built in 1839-41 on the north side of Goderich, overlooking the Maitland River. The jail itself is octagonal, with a central stairhall. The chapel on the top floor—which served initially as a courtroom—and the stairhall are lit by an octagonal lantern. An octagonal wall originally surrounded the whole. (One quadrant was later filled with a house connecting to the main block, for the warden.) A monumental entrance in the perimeter wall opens to a covered passage which converges as it leads to the central structure. From this, wings radiate on the so-called panopticon principle, allowing the turnkey to oversee all activity on one level by glancing down the radiating vistas. The system of separate blocks was supplemented by further walls between the core and the periphery to create separate exercise yards. The principle of both the blocks and walls was also humane in intention: to permit classification and separation of different types of prisoners on the basis of such features as sex, age, offence and recurrence. This general pattern was widely advocated in the first half of the nineteenth century in British literature, both architectural and official.[2] But few jails could have had the isolated clarity and geometric lucidity of this appealing example, and it is doubtful whether any other of the type is as well preserved.

The Lanark County Jail of 1862-63 in Perth (PLATE 77) is wholly different in structure and meaning. It stands behind the rather earlier Court House but, somewhat unusually, faces out to the parallel street on the other side of the block. Compositionally it is similar to the design for 'A Two-Storey Farm House' from the *Canada Farmer* (fig. 6) and the houses related to that design (PLATES 86 and 87). But the Jail is executed with boldly rusticated masonry, still more heavily treated in the rock-faced quoins, and poignantly played off against the thick, smooth window dressings with crisply-cut lozenges on the keystones. The bridge-like element at the base of the building leads to the administrative offices; it also gives access through the deeply-shaded portion beneath to the cells. When the Jail is compared with the contemporary Town Hall, the latter seems expansive and soft, the Jail constricted and tough. There is a quality of carefully-calculated excess in the Jail which makes it a masterpiece of what the eighteenth century called *architecture parlante*: architecture which speaks, as it were, so that it communicates its social meaning to the mind instinctively, through its visual form alone.

The grouping formed by a court house and jail is rarely complete without a county registry office, and in most cases this will date from the 1870s. The Lennox and Addington Registry Office at Napanee (PLATE 78) was built in 1871-72 and follows the uniform plan approved by Order-in-Council, 9 March, 1868. As Kivas Tully's appointment to Public Works as the first Architect and Engineer was finally confirmed on June 5th of that year, it seems likely that once again it was he who rose to the occasion and produced the design. The plans were lithographed and supplied by the Commissioner of Public Works for distribution to municipal councils.[3] According to the *Report of the Commissioner of Public Works* for 1869, only three registry offices had been completed by that date: St. Catharines,

Cobourg and Pembroke.

These uncomplicated-looking buildings are decidedly complex structurally, as they were intended to be fireproof. The doors, window-sills and lintels were cast-iron. Within a rectangular plan, three semi-cylindrical vaults of brick—technically barrel vaults—were constructed side by side, each nearly eighteen feet high and roughly two feet thick.[4] These were arranged to run across the width of the structure, generally with access through the first chamber to the clerk's office in the second, and with the storage vault in the third. The location of the separate compartments, though not their form, is often indicated on the exterior by panelling of the long side walls into three bays. The front end wall is generally treated as a blind arcade enclosing round-arched openings and fully-articulated orders, with trim in stone (as at Napanee) or patterned brick. The arcade is expressive but not, as one might think, a ghost of the vaulted interior, as the vaults are arranged transversely.

The typical Ontario school is a special case among public buildings. The earliest schools in the province were not, in fact, public; they were conducted in private homes. The Common School Act of 1816 provided limited grants toward the expenses involved in conducting schools with twenty or more pupils, but made no provision toward erecting or maintaining the structure. With the cost of their construction left to the community, the first school buildings tended to be of the simplest possible construction—small log or frame structures with a door in one end and a fireplace at the other, and a few windows down either side. Such schools were similar to log churches for the good reason that their requirements were similar: cheap construction, orderly exit, compact accommodation and adequate lighting.

Paradoxically, one of the earliest surviving educational buildings, the former Upper Canada Academy of 1832 at Cobourg (PLATE 17), was also one of the largest and grandest built anywhere in nineteenth-century Ontario. The cornerstone names Edward Crane as architect and builder. The Academy is of very direct Georgian design with repetitive windows ordered by string courses throughout, and grouped under pediments in the slightly projecting ends. Its site is splendid, at the top of a slope, commanding the long vista from the harbour—before the trees were planted—by its extraordinarily gawky Doric portico and domed cupola. The columns almost certainly replace earlier ones in the Ionic order, the traditional proportions of which are more nearly suited to the situation. Originally there was a further stage to the cupola, and W.H. Bartlett's view of Cobourg shows how strongly the whole building dominated the town.[5] Clearly it far surpassed Fraser's court house as the town's visual centre.

The School Act of 1846 facilitated the organization of local school boards and gave assistance in establishing schools. But there are few common denominators in schools like those in Williamstown (PLATE 25) or Milton (PLATE 45), except for a certain rangy quality dictated by lighting and circulation criteria.

On the other hand, the one-room schools in rural settings, dating from the 1860s or 1870s, conform to a careful program of use enunciated through the *Journal of Education for Upper Canada*.[6] This began publication in 1848 under Egerton Ryerson (1803-82) – the Methodist minister, founder and first principal of Upper Canda Academy – who was named Superintendent of Schools in 1846 (the year of the School Act), and George Hodgins (1821-1912), a pupil of Ryerson at the Academy who subsequently became Deputy Minister of Education. Ryerson and Hodgins combed other educational publications for suitable material to reprint and published much of their own. As early as January 1849, Ryerson and Hodgins started a series on school architecture in the *Journal of Education* with material excerpted from a well-known American book by Henry Barnard, *School Architecture; or Contributions to the Improvement of School-Houses in the United States*, a book which went through many editions after its first appearance in New York in 1841. Ryerson bought 400 copies of Barnard's book for 'each of the County, Township, City, Town, and Incorporated Village Schools, or School Corporations, in Upper Canada.'[7] Much of this material was then gathered in book form and published by Hodgins as *The School House; its Architecture* in 1857. The second edition of Hodgins' book in 1876 was a truly comprehensive compilation touching on every facet of the subject: the history and philosophy of schoolhouse architecture, siting and landscaping; designs for schools and their outbuildings; heating, lighting, plumbing and ventilation; furnishings and teaching aids (from pencil racks and book carriers to scientific apparatus and magic lanterns); even playground equipment and calisthenic exercises were covered.[8]

Some of Hodgins' designs look foreign to our eye and were, in fact, drawn from American sources, but his book is of unusual importance. Many original wood engravings were evidently borrowed from publishers in the United States. These must have struck contemporaries as equally exotic (not to say bizarre, in certain instances), since they were not used. But as against the plates in the first edition of the book, there were 'many additional ones (some of which are Canadian)' in the second. For this reason alone, the second edition would be

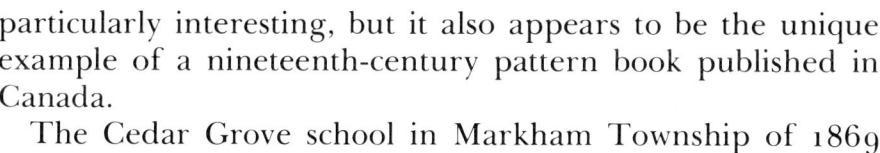

14

particularly interesting, but it also appears to be the unique example of a nineteenth-century pattern book published in Canada.

The Cedar Grove school in Markham Township of 1869 (PLATE 79) is an archetypal example—in siting and elevation, if not plan—of the use of those influential published designs, like that reproduced here (fig. 14).[9] This schoolhouse is set back farther from the road than usual and is also more remote from the hamlet it serves. But the educators were anxious that 'It should be sufficiently remote from the street or road to secure freedom from noise and dust, by which the attention is distracted, and time lost in cleansing soiled hands, faces and apparel. Ample play-grounds should be attached, because otherwise the attractions of sport would distract the children till the last moment, at places remote from the building . . . .' As for the schoolhouse itself, 'When practicable, the building should front south, with a dead wall to the north, and windows on the east and west. The light will then fall upon the pupil's right hand in the forenoon, and gradually pass around, till in the afternoon it rests upon his left hand, while during the whole day the eyes will be relieved, when lifted, by resting upon the dead wall in the north . . . . The teacher's platform should be at the front . . . for convenience in speaking with pupils as they enter or retire, conferring with visitors, securing order in entries, halls, etc.'[10] In fact, the Cedar Grove schoolhouse faces north and is provided with two more doors on the south, leading into cloakrooms and then into the schoolroom, but the children faced north as suggested. The windows to either side of the visitors' and teacher's entrance were for external appearance only, they were walled up just behind the plane of the glass.

Even the landscaping was specified and intended to be practical, useful and instructive, in keeping with Ryerson's philosophy of education. If the choice of site were open, 'a spot should be chosen upon which some large forest trees are already standing, or the border of a wood might be selected which could be easily thinned out.' Victorian society imputed moral grandeur as well as physical perfection to mature woods, and the *Journal* expressed concern that 'Generations must live and die before trees newly planted will assume that stateliness and beauty possessed by our ancient forest trees.' If, on the other hand, it were necessary to plant the trees, as at Cedar Grove, then some mixture of maple, locust, poplar, oak, sycamore, ash, beech, pine, cedar and hemlock was recommended and might be planted in accordance with a plan reproduced there. 'It will be observed that all those named are indigenous to our Canadian forests, and if the school-grounds were...planted with a variety of our most conspicuous and useful trees...the inquiring pupil might learn their names, classes and uses. The same principle should be applied in selecting shrubbery and flowers' so that 'pupils might learn useful practical lessons in the study of botany' as well as 'refine their taste.'[11]

In the 1880s the Dominion Government added an important series of urban structures which were truly landmarks: the Post Offices. All emanated from the office of Thomas Fuller (1823-1898), the English architect who had emigrated to Canada in 1856, won the competition for the Centre Block of the parliamentary complex at Ottawa in 1859, then worked extensively in the United States before returning to Ottawa as Dominion Architect in 1881.[12]

There is the strongest family resemblance among these government buildings, yet each was highly individual, with a character of its own, fitted to the peculiar nature of the town and its site. The example in Port Hope (fig. 15) was one of the earliest and most complex. The contract was signed 5 April, 1882 and the completed structure was dated 1883. Certainly it was the most exciting and distinguished of all these buildings by Fuller, but it was pulled down as recently as 1971. It was primarily of red brick, strongly banded horizontally, but picturesquely stepped, reflecting in these respects the disciplined but individual brick architecture of an earlier era on Walton Street, the main street of Port Hope (PLATE 1), just around the corner from the Post Office.

The old Almonte Post Office, standing at the head of Mill Street (PLATE 99), is typical of the simplest examples. They were designed as two-and-a-half-storey rectangular buildings with one-storey extensions at the rear. The longer face was turned to the street, taller than it was wide, and had a high gable in the centre. There was a door to either side, one for the Post Office and one for Customs. Fuller's manner was a distinctive combination of French Renaissance composition and High Victorian Gothic detailing—a forceful mixture of massively-proportioned blocks with roughly-textured surfaces, incorporating rhythmically-varied but strongly-grouped elements. The vista at Almonte is dominated by a facade of typical detailing: paired small windows under a round arch filled with checkerboard patterns; a larger pair of windows, each with a radially-patterned window-head enclosed by a thick band of stone work, and then a triad of very small windows topped off by the tough, *diamanté* or nail-head pattern in the gable.

The local character is expressed partly through the materials: the roughly-dressed sandstone from nearby North Elmsley was available in 'white, yellowish white or bright yellow, and the same colors, beautifully striped and mottled with dark purple.'

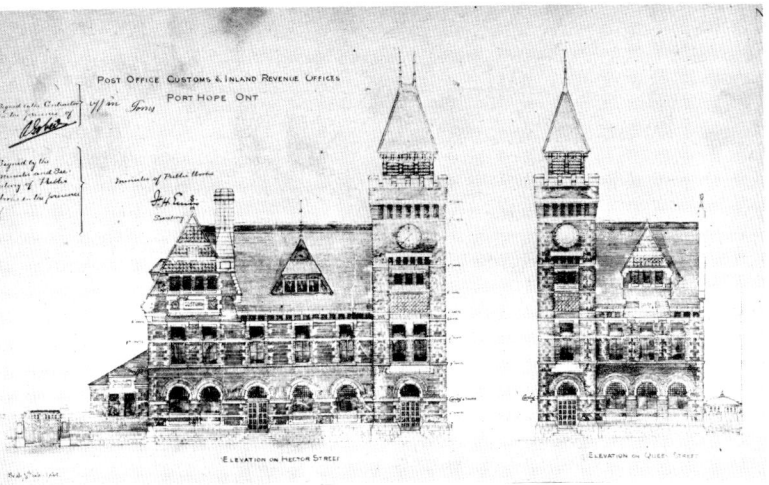

15

It is trimmed in this case with Nova Scotia red sandstone to enhance the plummy colour.[13] The characteristic design is also modified here to express the elevated site through the atypical use of an elaborately-detailed end wall complete with another gable, and the very visible, highly individual, clock tower.

Buildings like these were designed to last forever. Soundly designed, solidly constructed, they housed public services on the first floor and offices on the second, while an unfinished third floor provided space for future expansion. They represent some of the most individual and significant architecture in the community. In spite of this, many of them are endangered. The future of the Almonte Post Office, for example, is uncertain. In fact, the recent reorganization of the public sectors served by the various buildings described in this chapter and the provision of new, larger structures threaten most of these landmarks of the past.

[1] The maples are referred to as if recently planted in the text accompanying the illustration reproduced here from the *Canadian Illustrated News*, IV (19 August, 1871). 118.
[2] The widely-used English pattern book by [Peter Nicholson], *The New Practical Builder, and Workman's Companion* (London, 1823-[25]), includes an Irish example which is octagonal and has radiating wings – the County Cavan Gaol of 1810, by Richard Elsam. Others were illustrated in the Blue Books, the annual reports issued by the various boards of Public Works throughout the United Kingdom.
[3] *Report of the Commissioner of Public Works of the Province of Ontario, for the Year 1868* (Toronto, 1868), p. 7. It has not been possible, however, to locate a copy of the lithographed plans.
[4] A draughtsman's plan, longitudinal section and elevation of the Registry Office, Peterborough, Ont. in the Ontario Ministry of Government Services, Central Drawings File No. 2-69-1-4, confirms the details of construction.
[5] Both Bartlett's view, in N.P. Willis, *Canadian Scenery Illustrated*, II (London, 1842). facing 51, and that in William H. Smith, *Smith's Canadian Gazetteer* (Toronto, 1846), facing p. 34, show Ionic columns.
[6] Designs for larger schools, both primary and secondary, were also published in the *Journal*, But such schools seldom survive. The few remaining in towns were altered in appearance or use, e.g., the East Ward school in Napanee, now a warehouse, or the High School, Streetsville, which was subsequently a church and is now the Municipal Buildings.
[7] 'School Architecture in Upper Canada', *Journal of Education*, III (September 1850). 136.
[8] J. George Hodgins, *The School House: its Architecture, External and Internal Arrangements; with Elevations and Plans for Public and High School Buildings. Together with Illustrated Papers on the Importance of School Hygiene and Ventilation; also with Practical Suggestions as to School Grounds, School Furniture, Gymnastics, and the Uses and Values of School Apparatus* (Toronto, 1876).
[9] Curiously this design bears a very close resemblance to that of, not a school, but A Rural Church in the Plainer Romanesque Style by Connecticut architect Sidney Mason Stone in *A Book of Plans for Churches and Parsonages* (New York, 1853), design IV, published by the General Convention of the Congregational Churches in the United States. Ryerson, a Methodist, may well have had a copy of this handsome folio.
[10] From a report of Hon. N. Bateman, State Superintendent of Schools for Illinois, reprinted as 'How School-Houses Should be Constructed,' *Journal of Education*, XXII (July 1869). 97-98.
[11] 'Plan of the School Site, Trees, Shrubberies, &c.,' *Journal of Education*,

XXIII (March 1870). 38. The important plan of the school grounds (but not the text) had previously appeared in Hodgins, *The School House* (1857), p. 57.
[12] For biographical notices and short lists of works, see George Maclean Rose, ed., *A Cyclopaedia of Canadian Biography, Being Chiefly Men of the Time*, I (Toronto, 1886). 140-41; 'Thomas Fuller,' *Canadian Architect and Builder*, XI (October 1898). 168-69; and Henry F. Withey and Elsie Rathburn Withey, *Biographical Dictionary of American Architects (Deceased)* (Los Angeles, 1970), p. 226.
[13] Andrew Bell, 'Building Stones of Eastern Ontario,' *Canadian Architect and Builder*, IX (March 1896). 43.

COMMERCE, INDUSTRY & THE RAILWAY

Industrial and commercial architecture—apart from the simplest types of mills—was largely a development of the late eighteenth century. The appearance of new types of buildings for commerce, industry, and the railway, fascinated nineteenth-century observers. In July 1852, for example, the Toronto *Anglo-American Magazine* commented specifically on one of the new types—'the princely stores already built or in the course of erection' in the city. These were evidence of 'the wondrous metamorphosis of forty years,' during which 'every stone and brick has been placed in its present position, under the eye of many who remember the locality as . . . primeval woods.'

The principal problem in store architecture was to open large windows in the wall so as to display goods effectively and admit sufficient light to the single, deep, interior space. In a wooden structure, creating large openings was a simple task using the traditional heavy frame construction to span the openings. However, in one of the earliest surviving examples of a store building in the province the builder was timid: the display windows in the unusual complex at Martintown (PLATE 39), which may date from the 1840s, are scarcely larger than the doorways. But the store differs from a conventional house in that these windows are framed exactly like the doorcase—monumental forms to attract the eye.

The house and store at Waterdown (PLATE 40) possibly dates from the 1850s, and represents a more coherent and rational approach to the problem, even if the detail is rather summarily handled. The openings are grouped symmetrically in the gable end of the building. The doors (now glazed) and shop windows fill the whole surface area, but for points where structural supports are located. Paired, slender pilasters face these structural members and serve as symbolic supports in precisely the same manner as more fashionable shopfronts of the late Georgian period in Britain. But a quick, staccato rhythm is produced at Waterdown by the slight and brittle frame construction typical of North America.[1]

On the other hand, the house and general store in Camden East (PLATE 67) relies on no detailing whatever to organize the design or dramatize the public function. Its dual role is conveyed purely by the massing and distribution of openings, with large, fixed windows in the storefront containing larger-than-ordinary panes of glass. At the same time, it carries the mixed type of building a stage further in the dignified combination effected between the commercial and residential. The gable end with the store is similar to the Waterdown example, but more relaxed in feeling. The structure as a whole is singularly substantial, especially for a small community like this, and illustrates Anna Jameson's comment in 1837 that 'the grocery store, or general shop . . . in a new Canadian village is always the best house in the place.'[2]

There are many examples of later stores based on the picturesque house type of the T-shaped plan illustrated previously (fig. 6). By placing the building near the street and eliminating the bay window in the projecting wing, the builder could convert this near portion into a store and keep the set-back portion of the house with its small buffer of green space as the residence. Commercial architecture is generally associated with densely built-up areas, but the free-standing block which serves as both house and store is characteristic of the open and loosely-planned feeling of many Ontario towns.

Mills constructed of timber had appeared along the frontier in Upper Canada, often long before any settlement. The government, recognizing that settlement would be encouraged by providing for supplies of flour and lumber, built the first mills and had a monopoly on them for the first few years. In 1793, however, settlers were permitted to improve the water power on their own lots. (There were small mills driven by horses, and some windmills, especially in the Western District, but most mills drew their power from water.) By 1799 the Surveyor-General of the province counted between 30 and 40 mills along the St. Lawrence River between the eastern boundary and Kingston, a distance of about 120 miles.[3] At particularly choice sites with easily-accessible transportation, such as Merrickville on the Rideau Canal, a whole complex of mills would develop over the years (PLATE 35). The Rideau River drops more than 24 feet here and the island in the centre of the river, as well as the bank north of the island, provided ideal siting for mills and foundries in close association with the canal.

The mills tended to follow a narrow range of patterns until after the middle of the nineteenth century, regardless of the type of machinery housed or the end product. Grist, lumber and woollen mills were sometimes closely associated, as at Merrickville and the early mill site at Napanee sketched by Thomas Burrowes (fig. 16). Sometimes a mill changed functions over the years, but whether the power were supplied by an undershot wheel, an overshot wheel or – later – a turbine, scarcely affected the structure and appearance of the mill. As in the United States, early mills were generally all wooden. Stone construction – which was relatively common in the British Isles – came into use on this continent only in the early

Grist Mill, Saw Mills, &c. on the Nappanee River, at Nappanee Village.

nineteenth century as a precaution against fire, and came to be associated particularly with the later grist and woollen mills.

The plan of a mill was generally a rectangle, the width determined by the limits of timber framing and the length by the total square footage required per floor. Both wooden and stone mills were framed internally with two rows of massive posts, carrying immense squared beams and big joists. Since mills were dependent on a head of water, they were commonly set into a river bank, exposing more storeys to view in some elevations than others. In grist mills, each succeeding storey was generally taller than the one below it, for storage in the upper levels, to house the machinery, and to accommodate the long chutes required in processing the grain in a gravity-fed system. The columns were usually chamfered at the corners and roughly blocked at the top, giving the appearance of the traditional succession of orders – Doric, Ionic and Corinthian – each more elongated and slender than the one before. Very rationally, the walls in the stone mills were also thinned from formidable dimensions at the base, about four feet, to a thickness of about two feet at the eaves; sometimes the walls tapered, but frequently the change was abrupt, floor by floor, to provide for seating the floor joists. In elevation, the end wall might be very symmetrical, with a succession of loading bays extending up the centre to the gable as at Napanee. If the mill were built of stone, these bays would be deeply recessed in the thickness of the wall. The long walls, on the other hand, might have window openings as variable as the placement of the machinery inside suggested, particularly in the earlier mills. Later mills were extremely regular in appearance, as at Merrickville.

Mills rarely elicited comment. Sir Richard Bonnycastle mentions the mills at Gananoque in 1841 only because 'I was indeed surprised . . . to see such an establishment reared, as it were, in the bosom of the forest, and possessing machinery of the most expensive and complicated description.'[4]

The railway stations which began to appear in the 1850s represented a wholly new class of architecture and did excite attention. Like the one which formerly stood at Shannonville (PLATE 48), most of the stations on the Grand Trunk Railway line between Montreal and Toronto (completed in 1856) were built of stone or brick to a nearly uniform design.

They were very substantial-looking masonry buildings under low-pitched roofs with a marked overhang. The corners of the block were punctuated by four chimneys. There were five, six or seven round-arched openings in each long wall, and pairs in the ends, all outlined with large blocks, sometimes alternately long and short as at Shannonville. Externally the design was undifferentiated, as each opening extended to ground level and was fitted with French doors originally; inside, the four corners accommodated a general waiting room and a ladies' waiting room at one end, a baggage room and a storage room at the other. A lobby extended through the centre from front to back, and the telegraph and ticket offices lay between the lobby and the baggage-storage areas. Two surviving stations — Kingston and Belleville — have a second storey under a mansard roof.

The architect remains unidentified, but may have been Thomas S. Scott (died 1895).[5] He is principally remembered for the tall tower he later added to the West Block on Parliament Hill in Ottawa, but he was named as the Grand Trunk's architect in an advertisement in an apparently unique copy of the *Canadian Railway and Steamboat Guide* (3 September, 1858), for tendering on the line in Quebec from St. Thomas to Rivière du Loup. Pierre Gauvreau is also listed, and his office given as Quebec, while Scott's is Montreal. As the stations on that section are likewise uniform in design but markedly Québecois, it seems plausible that Gauvreau designed these while Scott did those west of Montreal.

The simple arcaded design of these Ontario stations has no close relationship to either English or American railway architecture. The germ is probably to be discerned in an idea, rather than a particular form, in R.M. Stephenson's small, early booklet, *Railways: an Introductory Sketch, with Suggestions in Reference to their Extension to British Colonies* (London, 1850). Stephenson illustrates four German railway stations, the smallest of which, that at Höchst (built about 1839), is reproduced here (fig. 17). He comments that 'The simple and economical character of the stations generally on the Continent and in America, are especially deserving of imitation, as structures which can at all times be enlarged, extended, altered, or rebuilt, without interruption of the traffic, and the ultimate dimensions and appliances of which cannot, in many cases, be determined until after the line has been for some time in operation.' Though none of the Ontario stations seems to have been enlarged in this way, one can appreciate the appeal of the concept as well as the round-arched form of the model.

The public took great interest in these Grand Trunk stations and objected to anything less fine. A.M. Ross, the GTR chief engineer, 'suggested that in order to meet the increased demand for Stations we should be allowed to construct ... in a less costly manner by the substitution of timber stations instead of stone or brick,' but 'the idea ... created ... so loud a clamour throughout the country generally, participated in by the representatives in Parliament, that the demand ... had to a large extent to be submitted to.'[6]

The contractors for the line from Montreal to Toronto were the British organization of Peto, Brassey & Betts; the line west of Toronto was built by the Canadian firm of Gzowski & Company. Walter Shanly, at the time chief engineer of the Western Section, wrote to his brother, Francis, from Prescott (1 December, 1855): 'The Grand Trunk buildings here are very well built, better than anything we can show.'[7] Nevertheless, several fine stone stations were built under the supervision of Shanly; only one, St. Mary's Junction, built in 1856, survives today.[8] The majority of stations west of Toronto were of frame, like those of other contemporary railways.

The Stouffville station, dating from the early 1870s (PLATE 92), illustrates the more complex massing in frame stations typical of the later nineteenth century. The waiting room is at one end of the structure and the station agent's office in the middle. The use of the telegraph in dispatching trains made the bay window a standard feature: it housed the telegrapher's box and gave the dispatcher a clear view of trains arriving and departing. The freight shed at the other end of the station can also be clearly distinguished as it is obviously different in character again. If agent's quarters were provided, they were on the second floor. There is a terseness characteristic of Ontario in these structures. But neither they nor the multi-turreted, hip-roofed stations of outrageously (and appealingly) romantic profile at the end of the century stand so clearly apart from contemporary American work as the early GTR stations.

The same combination of structural rationalism and visual romanticism may be discovered in the industrial and commercial structures of the last third of the century. Like the large textile mill at Campbellford (PLATE 93), more often than not these are brick buildings with facades subdivided vertically by big bands of projecting brick masonry. The bands correspond to the grid of internal supports, and enclose recessed panels in which the windows are grouped. In this instance, corbelled brickwork at the top of each recess, augmented by stone bands at the level of the window-sills, creates an equally potent horizontal accent that emphasizes the big, boxy volume of the mill.

William Fairbairn, the British iron master, took credit for the new kind of design. He noted that the earliest factories were simply 'square brick buildings, without any pretensions to architectural form,' but pointed out that 'About the year 1827, I gave designs for a new mill of a different class' with 'some deviation from the monotonous forms then in general use. This alteration had no pretension to architectural design; it consisted chiefly in forming the corners of the building into pilasters, and a slight cornice round the building.' Strangely, the engineer speaks only of 'the art of design' and the way 'it generally improved the appearance of the buildings, and produced in the minds of the mill owners and the public a higher standard of taste.'[9]

It was left to an architectural historian, James Fergusson, to point out the structural significance of a whole system of such architectural refinements. To the question 'What is architecture?' he answered as follows, using the diagram reproduced here of 'a cotton-factory, a warehouse, or any very commonplace utilitarian building' (fig. 18): 'The first division, A, is not only the most prosaic form of building, but is bad building, as no attempt is made to strengthen the parts requiring it, and no more thought is bestowed upon it than if it were a garden wall.... The second division, B, is better: the arching of the upper windows binds together the weakest parts, and gives mass where it is most needed to resist the... thrust of the roof; and... carrying down the piers between the windows gives strength where wanted. In this stage the building belongs to civil engineering..., the art of disposing the most suitable materials in the most economical but scientific manner to attain a given utilitarian end. In the third division, C..., the materials are better disposed... and even without the slight amount of ornament applied, it is a better example of engineering.... The cornice may be said to be required to protect the wall from wet; the consoles to support it; and the mouldings at the spring of the arch may be insertions required for stability. In the present day, however, even this slight amount of ornament is almost sufficient to take it out of the domain of useful art into that of architecture.' The fourth division, D, he considered entitled 'to rank as a work of the fine art' of architecture, simply because of the amount of ornament applied, even 'though it may be bad art.' In the fifth division, E, 'the parts are so disposed... to produce a more agreeable effect..., a better class of architecture than could be done by the mere application of any amount of ornament.' He concluded that 'architecture is nothing more or less than the art of *ornamental and ornamented construction*.'[10]

Clearly the Campbellford mill would rank as mere civil engineering, B, on Fergusson's scale, but a highly-ornamented structure like the Dundas cotton mill (PLATE 70), might rate a higher grade. Exceptionally in this most elegant—but now destroyed—mill, the brickwork is fully developed as a series of architectural orders, pilasters sitting on bases, and with capitals carrying a deep architrave. The whole system of slighter orders below is made up of cast iron—that building material which revolutionized nineteenth-century architecture. These iron columns carry the weight of the entire end wall. The window heads are also of cast iron and even the capitals of the upper

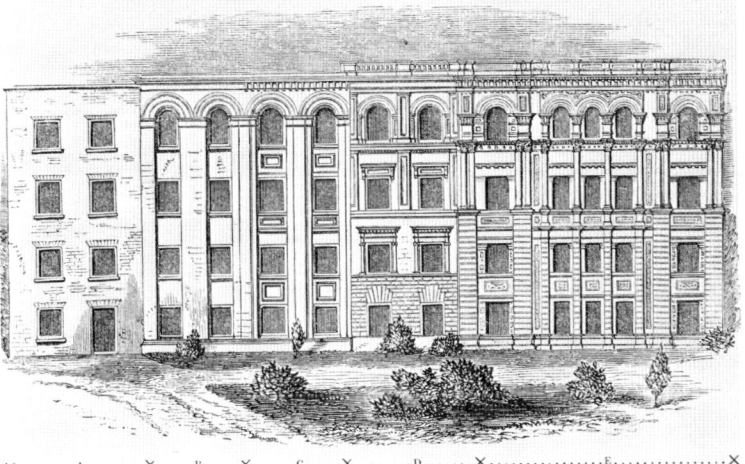

18

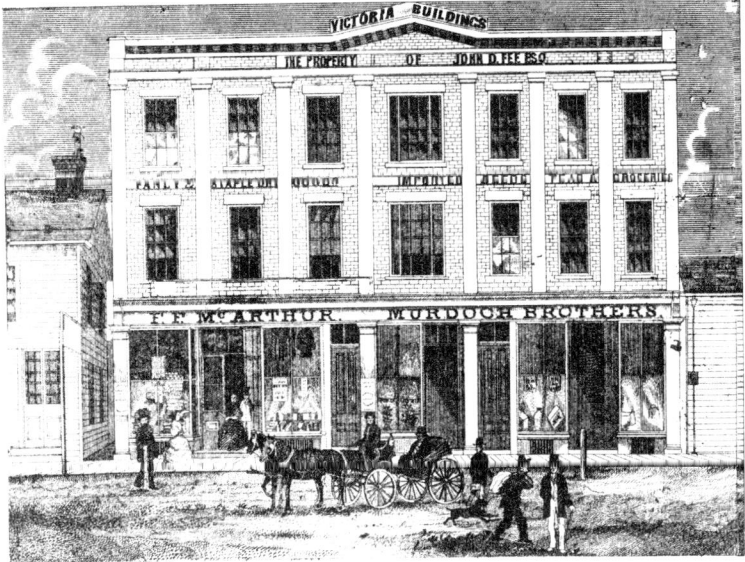

19

order are metal.

More significant than the refinement of the exterior surface, however, was the development of 'slow-burning' or 'true mill' construction characteristic of the interior structure of better North American textile mills in the second half of the nineteenth century. Penman's No. 1 Mill in Paris (PLATE 84) is a example of such construction. Instead of traditional floor construction with flooring laid on joists carried by the beams, large-dimension timbers—taking the place of both flooring and joists—were laid side by side on the beams to retard the spread of fire by eliminating the smaller members and the air spaces that occur between them in conventional construction. Incombustible cast-iron columns replaced the traditional wooden posts—on only two floors, in this instance.

In commercial construction there was a tendency toward more highly-ornamented design in the latter half of the century. It was rarely so rational or architectonic as industrial architecture, but showed a remarkable degree of urbanity. The Victoria Buildings in Bowmanville (fig. 19) illustrate the new ambitions of the 1850s. In the first place, the building is of brick, unlike its older neighbours, and at the new scale of the period. Here again cast-iron supports are evidently used on the ground floor to open up the facade completely. Immense sheets of glass fill the huge openings and give a stilted look to the brick superstructure. The second and third floors are grouped together and articulated by the use of a colossal order in every bay. The rhythm is quickened and the precariously-poised appearance intensified because only four of the orders are aligned from top to bottom in the whole length of this facade. The use of crested over-windows elaborately cast in iron (or stamped in tin) also caught on in this period, as in the St. Lawrence Hotel of 1858 in Port Hope (PLATE 68), and continued in some parts of Ontario nearly to the end of the century, as in Dundas (PLATE 69). But the more coherent and classicizing style typified by the Victoria Buildings in Bowmanville was a regional style centred on Port Hope (PLATE 1).

The most important commercial building in Merrickville is particularly interesting as an example of the new feeling for monumental form in combination with traditional structural methods. From the rear it appears as a handsome but unexceptional stone block of customary urban form (PLATE 75). It is L-shaped to fit its corner site, with parapets above the roof and paired chimneys to serve as fire breaks, an arched laneway connecting the enclosed yard to the street, and few windows in the end wall, against the day a neighbouring structure might be built. The principal face, however, gives lip service to new theoretical considerations such as Fergusson's while it also opts for belligerently modern textures (PLATE 76). The street faces are coarsely dressed and panelled in a stripped Classical grid of rock-faced masonry which organizes the distribution of windows and, together with the late nineteenth-century stained-glass window transoms, almost succeeds in concealing its basically early nineteenth-century composition and structure. The building is rounded at the corner to facilitate the flow of pedestrian traffic and to make an arresting feature at the main intersection of the town.

When one steps back from the individual buildings to gain a perspective on the total picture in the Ontario urban core, it is striking how much most towns changed around the middle of the century. A fascinating view of Oshawa made some time between 1841 and 1846 illustrates this (fig. 20).[11] It shows a main street like many throughout the province in the third quarter of the century, in transition from lower to higher density. The street is evidently rutted and muddy, but some rudimentary board walks appear. On the near side of the street, livestock are being driven past fenced yards. On the other side, the narrow gaps between the older houses with their long fronts parallel to the street are being filled with frame structures that turn a gable to the street. The use of the boomtown front or false front to cover the gable ends and give a more continuous appearance to the streetscape is clearly employed here, although few people would associate this common North American form with southern Ontario.

The fact that the accident of survival produces a very unbalanced view of architectural history is clearly brought home by comments from the mid-century which suggest the enormous quantity of frame construction—even on the main streets—that has perished. For although brick and stone were employed nearly from the beginning, they were used particularly for public buildings and it should be noted how few houses in these materials are tabulated by early observers. Thomas Rolph's *Statistical Account of Upper Canada* (1836) comments enthusiastically on Cobourg, for example: 'it contains a population of 1,300 persons. Its streets are remarkably clean—the houses regular and painted. There are three brick and five large stone houses.' To this he adds 'a fine stone wind-mill' and the stucco-covered brick 'Seminary' (Upper Canada Academy): ten masonry structures in all, then, in a town of 1300.

Perth, however, was a stone-built town, and the gaps on Gore Street there were filled up in the prevailing manner right to the edge of the River Tay and the Tay Canal (PLATE 34). The buildings continued to be constructed of the beautiful local

20

21

sandstone, even into the twentieth century, set to the property line, more or less uniform in height. If a third storey were wanted in a building abutting a two-storey neighbour, a very civilized and polite solution might be found in a half-storey with dormers in the low roof, or a more steeply-pitched mansard roof; in either case, the existing cornice line was maintained thoughout a group of buildings.

In some communities the new density was achieved through much wooden construction, which was an invitation to disaster; a town like Port Hope might emerge strikingly new after two major fires in January and February 1849, had reduced much of its main street to ashes. What followed was the highly unified rebuilding of the main street with more elegant versions of the Bowmanville Victoria Buildings lining both sides of the street. Close comparison with Tremaine's view of Walton Street, published in 1861 (fig. 21), indicates that there have been few substantial changes in more than a century, although meaningless and destructive alterations are now beginning to deface the street at an alarming rate.

Seaforth, too, was rapidly rebuilt (PLATE 97) following a still more devastating fire at a rather later date – 4 September, 1877. Twelve acres – virtually the entire business portion of the town – was burnt, but 'new impetus ... was thereby given to building operations ... to such an extent, that ... after the lapse of little over two years, the burnt district is again covered with buildings – not the cheap, wooden structures of the fatal 4th of September, but splendid modern business blocks of brick.' Once again a remarkable degree of consistency was obtained through the use of common materials (white brick) and common sight-lines (in terms of set-back and rooflines). But here variety in detailing from one building to the next establishes entirely individual identities down the length of the street. The keenness of the competition is best expressed in the Cardo Block, which served a variety of primarily public functions and thereby assured the owner's personal prestige: a music hall on the upper floor became the town's principal meeting place, while the high mansard roof with its still higher mansarded tower (looking distinctly like a fire hall) gave focus to the streetscape, and the clock at the top became a landmark visible from nearly all parts of town. Henry Belden, the geographer, was moved by such structures to comment, rather injudiciously, that "In fact, they are almost enough to cause residents of some more antiquated places to desire some such accident to happen to their own town, provided property-owners were well insured.'[12]

But it would be entirely misleading to suggest that the people of Ontario have lovingly inherited and faithfully preserved both the pattern of our towns and the fabric of our buildings from the nineteenth century. The carnage wrought in Fergus by the demolition of one single building—or as much of it as the Royal Bank of Canada owned—is apparent at a glance. The vibrant and vigorously-detailed Groves Block was sensitively sited at the principal intersection in town (PLATE 98), and its loss is felt whichever way one approaches the four corners (fig. 22). Many of the finest monuments in the history of Canadian architecture have been built by our peculiarly powerful chartered banks. Regrettably, in recent years they have seen fit to destroy much of the architectural heritage they created, including nearly all of the Victorian banks, believing—mistakenly in most cases—that the erection of the new building confers more prestige and amenity than preservation of the old.

Losses among commercial and industrial buildings have been especially severe and the townscape as a whole has suffered traumatically as a result. Look at the panorama of Port Hope, taken less than a hundred years ago (fig. 23); a comparison with the present scene shows how great are the changes that have occurred in three or four generations. Only the town hall and a few of the houses still survive; the dam, the millpond, the mills and factories—tannery, brewery, sawmill and turnery—have gone, and a small park takes their place along the river. The roundhouse and other buildings of the Midland Railway have disappeared. Vacant lots have replaced many buildings. The viaduct has been rebuilt and a second constructed. Near the harbour stands a refinery, and alongside it a large factory and foundry have been built and razed in the interim.

Yet some towns still maintain their character and identity. Cobourg, Niagara-on-the-Lake, Port Hope, Perth, St. Mary's all convey the impression of a stability derived from age and valued inheritance. The quiet dignity of these towns is the product of tradition and a very human scale of building. But this dignity is seldom preserved in modern changes and new construction. The towns are losing their identity; the impression of stability is illusory. The pattern is fast disappearing. Needlessly.

[1] Such designs were rarely reproduced in professional literature, but several appear in the remarkable English pattern book referred to previously: [Peter Nicholson], *The New Practical Builder, and Workman's Companion* (London, 1823-[25]), p. 575. Nicholson's book was unusual in that it illustrated work in relatively—or even very—advanced style, but projects which were, at the same time, on a small scale and therefore useful to the architect working in provincial or colonial areas. At least one Canadian architect—John Howard—is known to have used the book.
[2] Anna Jameson, *Winter Studies and Summer Rambles in Canada*, I (London, 1838). 68.
[3] [David William Smyth], *A Short Topographical Description of His Majesty's Province of Upper Canada in North America* (London, 1799), p. 13.

[4] Sir Richard H. Bonnycastle, *The Canadas in 1841*, I (London, 1841). 107.
[5] According to Hugh G. Jones and Edmund Dyonnet, *History of the Royal Canadian Academy of Arts* ([Montreal], 1934), p. 129. Thomas Seaton Scott was born in England in 1836 and did not come to Canada until 1863. He was first chief architect to the Dominion Government, 1871 to 1881. The dates of birth and emigration would seem to suggest another Thomas S. Scott as the GTR architect, but in view of the fact Thomas Seaton Scott's chief works included the old Union Station in Toronto and the old Bonaventure Station in Montreal, such a conclusion is improbable.
[6] Report of A.M. Ross, Esquire to the Hon. John Ross, President of the Grand Trunk Railway Company, 20 December, 1856, in *Statements, Reports and Accounts of the Grand Trunk Railway Company of Canada* (Toronto, 1857), p. 42.
[7] Quoted in Frank Norman Walker, ed., *Daylight Through the Mountain: Letters and Labours of Civil Engineers, Walter and Francis Shanly* ([Montreal, 1957]), p. 320.
[8] The date of this and all other structures in its division are given in *Grand Trunk Railway System: Bridges, Buildings, Water Stations, Fuel Stations, etc., and all Track Structures on Middle Division* ([1900]), p. 151.
[9] William Fairbairn, *Treatise on Mills and Millwork. Part II. On Machinery of Transmission and the Construction and Arrangement of Mills* (London, 1865), pp. 114-15.
[10] James Fergusson, *The Illustrated Handbook of Architecture: being a Concise and Popular Account of the Different Styles of Architecture Prevailing in All Ages and All Countries* (London, 1859), pp. xxvii-xxviii.
[11] Labelled 'Oshawa, C.W.,' the print (possibly unique) must postdate the union of the provinces in 1841, but this specimen was found bound into a copy of W.H. Smith, *Smith's Canadian Gazetteer* (Toronto, 1846).
[12] *Illustrated Historical Atlas of the County of Huron, Ont.* (Toronto, 1878), p. viii.

1 Walton Street, Port Hope, looking west from the bridge

Walton Street stands out among the main streets of Southern Ontario for the splendid urban harmony of its buildings. It was built, for the most part, in one decade, the 1850s. The almost uniform range of buildings seen here on the north side of the street is complemented by related groups on the south side. The unity is apparent despite the patchwork painting of the brick, an old practice that continues at an accelerated rate. The pedimented block on the north closes the vista up Queen Street; the effect must have been particularly striking and even monumental when this block retained its arched ground-floor openings. Walton Street winds up the hill, and continues farther up as Ridout Street until it merges eventually with the Toronto Road, now part of Highway 2.

2 *The White House, near Amherstview*

Of the handful of houses in the province said to date from the eighteenth century, The White House is unique in preserving its period detailing and character. Built in 1793 by William Fairfield, Sr., it represents an amalgam of three traditions: British, American Colonial and French Canadian. Fairfield was a Loyalist from Vermont, where clapboarded frame was the prevailing mode of construction. Two features, however, which point to French-Canadian influence are the gabled roof of unusual height and the extension of its eave to form a galleried veranda: in Ontario, two-storeyed porches of this sort were commonly a feature of hotels rather than houses. Some of the interior trim is closely modelled after English pattern books.

3 *Log house, Palmer Street, Guelph*

John Galt built the first house in Guelph, The Priory, a large log house of unusual refinement, in 1827. This later and much smaller house likewise consists of a centre block flanked by lean-to wings. Like The Priory and some other houses in the area, the logs have been left exposed – a practice which was most uncommon in Ontario, except in temporary or utilitarian structures. The beautifully-panelled door and long casement windows enhance the architecturally-conscious form of the house as a whole.

4 *The White Chapel, on Highway 49 north of Picton*

The oldest Methodist chapel in continuous use in the province, the White Chapel was built 1809-11. The land was donated by Stephen Conger, a Loyalist born in New Jersey. The church strongly resembles many of the American seventeenth-century meeting-houses, being roughly square in plan, two storeys high, and clapboarded. The interior, with its gallery at the rear and along two sides enclosing the raised pulpit with a sounding board, derives from the same source. The austerity of simple geometric forms and unornamented construction inherited from New England shaped the Ontario tradition at the outset.

2

5 The Macpherson house, Thomas Street, Napanee

Allan Macpherson's house, built in the late twenties, appears in a sketch of Napanee village made by John Burrowes and dated by him 1830. Except for the pilasters on either side of the doorway, the south front appears in the sketch very much as it does in this photograph. Macpherson had lived at Kingston, but came to Napanee in 1812 to run mills owned by the Hon. Richard Cartwright. Porches were added later to the identical north and south fronts, and the pilasters are vestiges of these. The flues from no less than nine fireplaces are gathered into the three visible chimney-stacks; two of these fireplaces are in basements, and there are two bake-ovens—one in the kitchen in the wing, and the other in the basement at the opposite end of the house.

6 The Spencer house, Spencer Street East, Cobourg

This house is said to have been built by John Spencer, sheriff of Northumberland County, who owned the whole farm lot on which it stands and was living there before 1820. In 1829, shortly before his death, he was assessed for a two-storeyed house with five fireplaces, probably built on this site the previous year, when he had already begun to sell off the southern part of his property as lots for the expanding village of Cobourg. The slenderly-proportioned porch and the entrance with transom and side-lights are characteristic features of Regency style, but the paired bay windows reflecting the same influence are uncommon in Upper Canada.

7 The Barnum house, on Highway 2, west of Grafton

The well-known house built by Colonel Eliakim Barnum is the most superb translation of late eighteenth-century English style into wood. Said to date from 1817, it could not have been completed before 1819, as no two-storey house was assessed in Haldimand Township before 1820. Barnum came from Vermont, but his builder may have come from upstate New York, where similar houses are found—rarely, if ever, so fine. The most remarkable feature is the arcading of the entire facade, in which the exquisite contrast of one shallow plane against another is rendered with flush boarding. The same crisp, linear quality is achieved on the sides with traditional clapboarding, and the whole banded together by an unusual Doric frieze.

8 The Webster house, King Street West, Cobourg

Houses with their gables to the street were convenient on narrow town lots, where there was seldom room for even a wing to the side and any extension had to be toward the back. Such houses had become common by about 1840. This house, now mutilated, is an early example, which can be compared in plan and in the treatment of the gable with the centre part of the Barnum house. Until 1973 it retained the central chimney-stack, with four flues separated above the roof, and an early doorway (hidden by the later porch). The early roughcast house of classic simplicity was handsomely married to the board and batten porch with the flamboyant Gothic detail peculiar to this area.

9 The Wilderness, King Street, Niagara-on-the-Lake

When this house was finished by Colonel William Claus, it stood on the western outskirts of Niagara. It was romantically-sited like a Regency villa at some distance from the road in spacious grounds. It has kept its secluded position on a well-treed, four-acre plot. The older part of The Wilderness was built about 1816-17, and the wing to the right added later. The French doors at the left increase the asymmetrical aspect and provide the intimate connection with the grounds characteristic of Regency houses. The house is said to have been built in imitation of Longwood, on St. Helena, where Napoleon died. Longwood, however, is later in date, and the story likely arose from the fact that both houses are long, low, one-storeyed and rambling.

10 House, Gage Street, Niagara-on-the-Lake

Little is known about the origin of this house; it may date from the 1830s. The three-bay front is more common from about 1840, but the delicacy of the entrance suggests an earlier date, as does the placement of the window sash close to the outer surface of the wall with little or no outside reveal. The upper windows are shorter than the lower, having eight-pane sash above twelve-pane (twelve over eight would have been more usual), presumably because of the veranda roof, which can still be traced on the wall.

9

11 *Doorway, Breakenridge house, Mississauga Street, Niagara-on-the-Lake*

John Breakenridge, a lawyer from the Southern States, built himself 'several of the most elegant and tasty houses in town' according to his obituary in 1828. There is no doubt that this house was one of the finest in the rebuilding which followed the destruction of the town in the War of 1812. Strongly-moulded pilasters with tight Ionic capitals support a stilted overdoor with a complicated, deeply-projecting cornice. The scheme reproduces in miniature the articulation of the whole house with its colossal pilasters, two of which tightly frame the door. The fanlight shows the intricacy characteristic of English late Georgian work and New England Federal style; it is distinguishable from both in having an unfocused quality. The compartments are made of lead glazing bars punctuated with cast lead ornaments and festooned with swags.

12 *Houses on Queen Street, Niagara-on-the-Lake*

The length of a surveyor's chain – 66 feet – was commonly used to determine the width of streets in Ontario towns. Queen Street and five other streets in Niagara-on-the-Lake are, exceptionally, a chain and a half in width. The open feeling that this generous street allowance produces was complemented by the allocation of one-acre plots to the original settlers. When these houses were built in the early 1820s, the inhabitants clearly expected the town to become a major centre, and built windowless end walls so that other houses might be built adjoining. The arcaded brick house, with its stepped gable end to serve as a fire wall, is possibly the finest early example of a town house in Ontario. The rest of the row failed to materialize, and the open pattern persisted.

13 *Roslyn Cottage, Queen Street, Niagara-on-the-Lake*

The way in which Roslyn Cottage is built right on its lot line is very striking. It suggests that an older foundation was used in rebuilding this house about 1822. Like the Breakenridge house, it has colossal Ionic pilasters on the wall to the street. A Greek Revival veranda and doorway were added more than a decade later on the garden front. The detailing of the doorcase is taken from a plate in *Beauties of Modern Architecture*, a pattern book published in 1835 by the American architect, Minard Lafever.

12

14 *St. Andrew's Presbyterian Church, Niagara-on-the-Lake*

St. Andrew's was begun in 1831, and is the unique example in Ontario of a church based upon a pattern-book design. The brick body and wooden tower were derived from the sixth edition of *The American Builder's Companion*, 1827, by Asher Benjamin. Benjamin's design was updated, however, by the use of a classic Greek order of almost archaeological correctness for the portico. The specifications called for it to be built in 'Cooper's Doric,' the work presumably of James Cooper, a member of the congregation. The plan of the interior is again Benjamin's, but places the superb black walnut double-decker pulpit against the inner wall of the vestibule, and ranges the U-shaped gallery around the outer walls. St. Andrew's, with its spacious setting, is one of the finest monuments of its time and place.

15 *The Peck house, Dibble Street West, Prescott*

The number of houses in Ontario with full-scale Greek Revival porticos is very small. Most of them, like this house, date from the later 1840s. The type with two-storey temple front between one-storey wings was publicized by Minard Lafever in his pattern book, *The Modern Builder's Guide*, first published in New York in 1833. But the Peck house shows lingering elements of Georgian style, as in the insistent quoins which break the smooth stucco surface and disturb the geometric purity expected in Greek Revival work.

16 *The Alpheus Jones house, Dibble Street West, Prescott*

The Alpheus Jones house was first assessed in 1834, but must have been finished by 1833, when Jones wrote a recommendation for the masons who had been responsible for the stonework. The masonry is particularly fine, with the dressed ashlar front and rusticated corners and window jambs. The doorway is a remarkably well-designed example of the elliptical sort—a characteristic Ontario motif from the 1820s to the 1840s. The window above it, however, seems rather unhappily divided. The breaking of the string-course over the doorway may have been intended to allow for a pillared porch which would echo the upper pediment very pleasantly. Behind the house are extensive stone stables, coach houses and sheds. Alpheus Jones was postmaster of Prescott for many years, and a partner in an iron foundry.

17 Old Victoria College, from College Street, Cobourg

The cornerstone of the Upper Canada Academy was laid in 1832. In 1841 this Methodist Institution was rechartered as Victoria College, with power to grant degrees. Victoria University moved to Toronto in 1892, and this building is now used as a hospital. Edward Crane is given as architect and builder on the cornerstone. In the 1830s Greek Revival style was just coming into favour in Upper Canada. Here the three storeys are of brick on a stone basement, covered with stucco which was originally treated to resemble marble—as in some Greek Revival work in the United States—but is now painted white. The portico shows the attenuation of proportion noticed by contemporaries as a characteristic fault of 'Grecian' work in North America. The building is, in a severe way, decidedly handsome.

18 Terrace, Walton Street, Port Hope

This handsome terrace is an outstanding example of a distinctly urban type of building, which—outside the large cities of Ontario—is nearly unique to Port Hope. Its pilasters (executed in brick as in the commercial buildings on Walton Street), heavy entablature punctuated by small, oblong windows in the frieze, and eared trim on the nearer doorway are all typical features of Greek Revival style. The problem of accommodating a long building on rising ground is handled by adjusting the sill heights and floor levels. The effect of these differences is minimized by the common entablature and by the pilasters, which, being irregularly-spaced, give an unclear idea of the internal division of the terrace.

19 Bluestone, Dorset Street East, Port Hope

Bluestone was finished in 1834 by John David Smith, the son of Elias Smith Sr., who in 1800 laid out Smith's Creek, the village which became Port Hope. Bluestone, like the Macpherson house at Napanee, has two entrance doors—one facing south and the other, shown in the picture, to the north. The house has a more complete range of detailing—the bracketed cornice, moulded architrave under the eave, and fluted Ionic columns in the porch—than is customary in the first half of the nineteenth century in Ontario. Nevertheless, Bluestone is basically a rectangular, symmetrical Georgian house, carefully proportioned but supplemented with Greek details.

18

20 *St. Andrew's Presbyterian Church, Colborne*

A Book of Plans for Churches issued in 1852 by the Congregational Churches in the United States contained several designs in the Tuscan version of the Italianate style. The history of this Ontario example is somewhat complicated. The church is dated 1830 on the tower, while a spire is known to have been completed in 1832-33. The present belfry stage was built in 1910, but is such a successful example of vernacular Tuscan that it seems likely to have followed an earlier model.

21 *Huron County Jail, Goderich*

Huron County Jail was built in 1839-41 on land obtained from the Canada Company. It is an octagonal building with pediments on alternate faces which project slightly, and is crowned with a simple octagonal lantern lighting a circular stairhall at the centre of the building. The building is surrounded by an octagonal wall, part of which was removed to make room for the warden's house. The strongly-patterned portal, with its fine stonework, leads to a passage with sides converging on a smaller inner doorway, thus exaggerating the length by false perspective, a sophisticated device sometimes used in Renaissance architecture. The early assizes were held on the third floor, but the judges complained so bitterly at having to enter the court through the prisoners' quarters that it was removed to a local hotel until the new Court House was finished in 1856.

22 *Prince Edward County Buildings, Picton*

In 1831 the legislature of Upper Canada passed an act setting off the 'County of Prince Edward into a separate District'; hitherto it had formed part of the Midland District. It was, however, not until 1832 that tenders were called for the court house and jail at Picton, on land donated by the Reverend William Macaulay. Work began the same year, and it was completed by April 1834. Sited on a small rise, the building is extremely satisfactory in its proportions and design. Close inspection, however, suggests that it is essentially a finely-executed large house to which a colossal portico of equally smooth and simple form, and a cupola of almost onion-domed profile, have been added.

21

23   Old Church of St. Mary Magdalene, Picton

The Reverend William Macaulay, an independently wealthy Anglican missionary to Marysburgh Township, built a brick church in 1825-27 on his property adjoining what is now Picton harbour. Around the church he laid out a village plot which he named Picton. In 1837 this village was united with the larger community of Hallowell across the harbour to form the town of Picton. The four large windows in the body of this old church represent Macaulay's building. The shallow pitch of the roof and the glazing of the old windows with switchline tracery and clear glass are typical of the early period. The original tower was demolished, the nave extended slightly in stone at either end, and the massive tower added in a compatible though more advanced style—with diagonal buttresses and broached spire. The church is now out of use, and since the photograph was taken the windows have been boarded up.

24   The Newburgh Academy, Newburgh

Newburgh Academy was probably established in 1839. In 1853 the original building was replaced by a larger one, which burned in 1872. The present building is evidently a reconstruction of the latter within the same stone walls—a long, plain rectangle emphasized by a deep base-course, big quoins, and the strong line of the stone cornice. In the rebuilding a Gothic gable with frail bargeboards and cusped window was placed above the stern pair of Classic pilasters which frame the entrance. The result is a strong and handsome example of Ontario vernacular; sadly, it too is disused.

25   Former Grammar School, Williamstown

The Williamstown Grammar School was built in 1860, apparently for $1200. Its headmaster was Donald McLean, who had a bachelor's degree from Queen's University, Kingston; 40 pupils were enrolled. In some ways the brick building, with three sets of doors, resembles row houses of the period. Both the entrances at either end of the building and that in the centre are set between stripped Classical pilasters for emphasis. The effect is strongly patterned, and the patterning extends to the herringbone treatment of the window heads. The school is now a museum devoted to the history of the North West Company.

26 *Holy Trinity Anglican Church, Chippawa*

In July 1840, John Howard designed this remarkable Anglican church to replace one burnt the previous year. Holy Trinity, completed in 1841, is the Canadian equivalent of English 'Gothick' of the Georgian period. There is the same playful mixture of gothicizing elements—pointed arches, switchline tracery and crenellated parapets—superimposed on a Classical form strongly outlined by huge quoins and oversailing horizontal cornice. Even though Howard was a London-trained architect (who had come to Canada in 1833) he used mid-eighteenth-century conventions, as did the anonymous builders and architects of the province; he did so, however, with considerable sophistication—almost panache.

27 *St. Andrew's Presbyterian Church, Williamstown*

French-Canadian and English influences are both apparent in this Scotch kirk. Begun in 1812, its construction was interrupted by the War, and it was not completed until 1818. The masons were French-Canadians, which explains the Québecois appearance of its high walls of coarse rubble with very wide mortar joints. Likewise, the bell-tower is a French-Canadian *flèche:* the octagonal belfry sits angle-wise on a small pyramidal roof, and has a flared spire topped by a chanticleer weathervane. The windows, on the other hand, are an elaborate variant of an English Palladian motif; the conventional round-headed panel between narrow, square-headed lights is topped here by a glazed segment. The porch and massive decorative truss in the gable are additions of a high quality—which date from the 1870s when the interior was entirely remodelled.

28 *Riverest, L'Orignal*

Although John Marston was a Yankee, his house—splendidly sited on the right bank of the Ottawa River—is another successful blend of French-Canadian and English influences. As at St. Andrew's, Williamstown, coarse rubble masonry is found together with Palladian windows in profusion. Essentially, though, Riverest is a fine example of an early Ontario cottage with a hipped roof extending over the deep veranda, which once encircled the body of the house.

29   *The Baltimore Hotel, Division Street, Cobourg*

This is the last survivor in Cobourg of several early taverns of this general type: the two-storeyed inn with galleried veranda. The Baltimore Hotel appears to date from about 1830 or even a little earlier. The doorway opening onto the upper gallery is more elaborate than the lower entrance; there is headroom for an elliptical fanlight in the former case, but only a rectangular transom in the latter. The upper posts are probably original, but the lower ones may have been replaced. Some of the second-storey and attic sash has also been renewed.

30   *Inge-Va, Craig Street, Perth*

According to the Reverend William Bell (*Hints to Emigrants*, 1824), the first stone house in Perth was being built 'by one of our merchants' in the summer of 1823. Inge-Va is also said to have been built in 1823 – by the Reverend Michael Harris, the Anglican rector. The plane of the glass in the lower windows and doorway is flush with – and the cases actually in front of – the face of the stonework. This is a feature found in the early houses of this province; later the doorway would certainly have been recessed to the depth of the wall. The 'peak', with its long, arched window over the front door, was added later to light the upper hall. The house is celebrated for its connection with the last fatal duel fought in Upper Canada. This took place about a mile away between Robert Lyon and John Wilson in 1833; Lyon, mortally wounded, was carried to this house, where he died.

31   *The Matheson house, Gore Street East, Perth*

The imposing stone house built by Roderick Matheson in 1840 is still a dominant feature of the main street of Perth. In 1966 it was saved from demolition and has become the local museum. The dignity of the house results from careful, workmanlike handling overall, rather than from individual detailing. The use of a wide, extremely shallow, projecting centrepiece is a feature of English mid-Georgian architecture, found in earlier houses such as The Grange (1818) in Toronto. The Matheson house provides a refreshing break in Perth's commercial core; at the same time, its stone wall topped by handsome ironwork carefully maintains the street line.

32   St. John's Roman Catholic Church, from Brock Street, Perth

St. John's Church was completed in 1848. It is a simple stone edifice with boldly-modelled square towers projecting slightly across the front, and a series of pinnacled buttresses along the sides. An old print of Perth dated 1874 shows the church with only the square stone towers; the broached spires, of excessively spiky quality, are evidently later additions, but certainly always intended. They give the church an almost cathedral, yet toy-like, quality. The doorways are entirely modern alterations, but fortunately the superb interior—with beautifully-detailed arcades and plaster vaults—is well preserved.

33   View on Gore Street, Perth

There are several fine stone buildings of mixed commercial and residential use on the main street of Perth. This, at the corner of Harvey Street, is incomparably the most beautifully detailed. The ashlar masonry with its carefully rusticated openings may be compared with the Matheson house. This stone block, however, would appear to have been a terrace of three units originally, having a particularly dignified house in the recessed centre, while both wings probably contained stores. This is suggested by the length of the larger window in the ground floor of the left wing. In spite of ham-fisted alterations to this wing—and the more compatible changes to the store in the right wing—the total effect is still extremely striking. The large Mac-Martin house beyond offers a nice contrast in brick.

34   Gore Street and bridge over the Little River, Perth

Perth was laid out on either side of the Tay River where it divides and forms a branch, the Little River, which rejoins the Tay a few hundred yards downstream. A creek runs between the two, creating Cockburn and Haggart's Islands in the centre of the town. The stone bridge carrying the main street over the Little River follows a pattern which is centuries old: widespread pointed arches and—on the far side—a cutwater between them projecting upstream to break the force of the current. Beyond this, an attractive park straddles the stream. The combination of stone buildings, green spaces and running water gives Perth its unique character.

33

35 Mills, Merrickville

The first sawmill built at Merrickville by Roger Stevens in 1793 was on the south bank of the Rideau River, as was the grist mill built later by William Mirick. In all probability the site 'near the falls' was very close to these buildings, which stand on an island in the river. The long, tall building was clearly built in three stages. The earliest section—to the left, with small windows—served as a grist mill. The keystone over the main door of the central portion, a woollen mill, bears the inscription 'S.H. Mirick/1848'—Stephen Mirick was a son of William. The small stone building in front of the large complex was once a foundry. These buildings formed only part of a once-thriving industrial village, which owed its importance and prosperity to the canalization of the Rideau. This fine mill structure is threatened and has already lost its roof and belfry.

36 Farmhouse near Easton's Corners

Two building materials are characteristic of the Merrickville area: stone and—less frequently—a combination of red and yellow brick laid in a distinctive pattern, as in this house near Easton's Corners. The walls are laid up in Flemish bond, with bricks laid alternately lengthwise and crosswise in every row. All the lengthwise brick is red; the rest is yellow. (The reverse pattern is also found in the area.) The entrance is of the elliptical type popular in the second quarter of the century, but the narrow lancet in the peak and the heavy trim at the eaves are indications of its later date; it is said to have been built in 1858.

37 Mennonite Church, Altona

In 1853 the Society of Mennonists built this lovely little church in the hamlet of Altona. It is built in the delicately-coloured local brick of a shade between oatmeal and salmon-pink. This characteristic Mennonite church is not unlike a Quaker meeting-house. But while the Mennonites segregated the congregation four ways—men, women, boys and girls—they did not insist upon separate entrances for men and women, as did the Quakers. Here, the door in the centre provides direct access to the church proper, and the other door leads to a vestibule across the end of the building. The interior of this church is particularly well-preserved and the churchyard contains many interesting stones.

38   Bethel Chapel, Britannia Road, near Kilbride

Bethel Chapel was built in 1853 by the Canadian Wesleyan New Connexion, a Methodist sect. The repetitive horizontal rhythm of the clapboarding sets off the massive doorway of mid-century character with extensive flat planes picked out by boldly-projecting mouldings. The symbolism of the entrance plays an important role in Christian churches—'I am the door: by me if any man enter in, he shall be saved'—nowhere more clearly than here.

39   Store building, Martintown

This most attractive little store building is part of an astonishing complex in the small village of Martintown. The group consists of a main block resembling a house, and a range of these stores forming an ell or tail. Possibly dating from the 1840s, this unaltered portion is, in any case, an early form of commercial architecture; the display windows are of characteristically modest proportions, and fitted with classicizing trim precisely like the doorway.

40   Store and house, Waterdown

This represents the characteristic Ontario store of the mid-nineteenth century, combining premises and residence in one building. What would otherwise be an ordinary house is set with the gable end close to the street, and the shop fills this portion of the ground floor. Both the individual panes and the windows themselves are much larger than in earlier stores such as those at Martintown. The spaces beneath the windows are panelled, and the pilasters between the openings are paired. The storefront is treated as a colonnade, and filled with as much glass as possible. The windows in the upper floor are widely spaced because they are centred over those on the ground floor, accounting for the austerity and yet the sense of order in this distinguished example of a class of buildings now nearly vanished.

39

41   *Porch, Lynnwood, Simcoe*

This is the handsome entrance to Lynnwood, a house built about 1851 by Duncan Campbell, then postmaster of Simcoe. It is analogous to, though richer in character than, the portico on the earlier Sovereign house in neighbouring Waterford (PLATE 43). Both are Greek Revival, but whereas the Sovereign house has an open portico with two severe Doric columns, Lynnwood has an enclosed porch, with four columns in the richer Ionic order, and a doorway with pilasters and arched architrave, as well as a tablet with a palmette acting as a pediment.

42   *The Sowden house, Burwell and Church Streets, Paris*

Dr. Sowden's house is one of a number of well-known cobblestone buildings in and near Paris. Cobblestone was introduced to this area by the builder, Levi Boughton, who came from upstate New York, where such construction with water-washed oval stones laid in regular courses is more common. Dr. Sowden is said to have built this house in the early 1840s, but the effectively-handled street corner (with an entrance presumably to his office), the bracketing under the eaves, and the detailing of the wide doorway, all suggest a date more than a decade later. Cobblestone patterning is reserved for the street fronts, the back and side walls being of ordinary fieldstone. Isolated examples of cobblestone masonry are found elsewhere in Ontario, but Sydney Township in Hastings County is the only other area in the province where there is a group of such buildings.

43   *The Sovereign house, Waterford*

Five-bay houses such as this, with two pairs of close-set bays and a wider bay in the centre, were built in most parts of the province until well after the middle of the nineteenth century. The type could be adapted to changing taste, to some degree, by altering the proportional relationships of individual elements and employing distinctive detailing. The Sovereign house, built on the outskirts of Waterford in 1842, reflects the influence of the Greek Revival in its sense of big scale and its bold detail. This massive quality is reinforced by the heavy cornice enclosing everything, including the four pairs of chimneys, and the plump balustrade on the low, hipped roof.

42

44 Town Hall, Dundas

Dundas once rivalled Hamilton as a flourishing lake port and manufacturing centre. After it was incorporated in 1847, no time was lost in planning a suitable town hall. A design by Francis Hawkins, a local builder, was accepted; work began in 1848 and the building was completed by July 1849. The Town Hall is one of the few municipal buildings surviving from before 1850, and one of the most effective. Though the building is inconsistently detailed in general, the pilasters unconventionally handled, and the pediment curiously scaled, it has more originality and strength than more sophisticated examples of Greek Revival style elsewhere. The wing projecting to the left is a later addition, and the entrance at its base is later still.

45 Bruce Street Public School, Milton

This school was built in 1856 by Messrs. Dodge and Hamburg from drawings by F.G. Dunbar to serve SS No. 5, Trafalgar Township. According to the minute book, the cost was almost £1500, including £3 each for two privies! Two wings were added in the early 1880s, more than trebling the size of the building without disturbing its simplicity. In fact, the masons closely matched the character of the rough stonework and even adopted the straight window heads of the original building in the street face of the new wings, although they gave the flank windows segmental heads and used fine-dressed masonry for the chimneys. The bellcote was almost certainly added at the same time as the wings—its form apparently inspired by the Italianate bracketing under the eaves. For no good reason, this fine school was demolished in 1973.

46 United Church, Actinolite

This former Wesleyan Methodist Church was built in 1864-66 in the village then known as Bridgewater. In addition to lumbering, the village was noted for its marble quarries, and this church is reputed to be the only one in Canada built of marble. It was designed by A.J. Stapely of Belleville. On 24 May, 1889, while most of the villagers were celebrating the Queen's birthday at Madoc (which had become a more important centre owing to the railway), a fire destroyed much of Bridgewater. The church had to be re-roofed, but the steeple and gallery were never replaced.

47 *Christ Church, Lakefield*

Kivas Tully was obviously enamoured of the mediaeval ideals of High Church architects in Britain when he designed the first Anglican church in Lakefield, built in 1853-54. In contrast to earlier churches in Ontario, the plan and profile of this church are complex, a relatively steeply-pitched roof, with a bellcote on the gable, sits on low walls, with a narrower, lower chancel at one end, and an even lower porch jutting out asymmetrically to one side. Diagonal buttresses increase the picturesque appearance. Christ Church nicely illustrates the principle of A.W. Pugin, the champion of the Gothic Revival, that 'all ornament should consist of enrichment of the essential construction of the building.'

48 *Former Grand Trunk Railway station, Shannonville*

Until it was demolished, this little station was the best surviving example of the many fine stone stations of simple Italianate design built in the mid-1850s on the Grand Trunk line between Montreal and Toronto. Only Shannonville remained virtually unaltered even to the chimneys. These stations were built by the English contractors, Peto, Brassey & Betts. Although the Canadian engineers and contractors, who were responsible for the line west of Toronto, were both suspicious and critical of the English consortium, they built several stone stations of similar design, one of which still survives at St. Mary's Junction, though it is now derelict.

49 *The Tracey house, Church Street, St. Mary's*

A log house built by George Tracey on this property in 1841 has been called the first building in St. Mary's, but his land was outside the village plot then and for some years after. This stone house was built by Tracey by 1850. Although it probably possessed some Gothic features from the first, it seems likely that the original design was more Classical than at present. The steep-pitched gables and grouped, diagonal chimneys very likely are original, but the richly-moulded and looped bargeboards, so typical of American pattern-book Gothic, seem like a later attempt to bring the house into fashion. As in several Gothic houses of the 1840s, the windows and verandas follow the older Classical forms, and it is unlikely that the handsome Gothic trimmings, rarely found before 1850, would have been combined with these quite un-Gothic features from the outset.

50 *Pinehurst, Pine Street, Port Hope*

The 'Tudor' style was all the rage for smaller houses in the British Isles during the 1830s and 1840s. Pinehurst, built in 1846, resembles the spiky, bald designs popularized by the Scottish writer, J.C. Loudon, in his *Encyclopaedia of Cottage, Farm, and Villa Architecture* (first published in 1833). Typical of such designs are the small, stepped gables barely large enough to hold the thickly-moulded, square-headed windows, and the thin pieces of tracery used to gothicize the windows. The enclosed porch, although practical in Ontario's climate—winter or summer—is relatively rare in this province, and the use of one here adds to the British appearance of Pinehurst.

51 *The Cone, Dorset Street West, Port Hope*

The Port Hope *Weekly Guide* of 25 September, 1858 described this board and batten house as 'a Villa erected upon the model of the Swiss Cottage, which promises to be, when completed, a perfect Gem.' Thomas C. Clarke, associate engineer of the Port Hope, Lindsay & Beaverton Railway, was the owner and, the *Guide* said, 'we presume, likewise the architect.' The site was described as 'one of the most beautiful in Port Hope . . . upon the brow of a fine slope . . . dotted with majestic trees' with 'a fine plot for an ornamental garden' at the foot of the hill. Only the right wing seen here is the original; the left wing was added some twenty years later. Originally the roof was 'covered with shingles, plain and scalloped,' which were 'disposed in bands.'

52 *The Rectory, Ontario Street, Collingwood*

All Saints' Rectory, completed in 1878, was based on the plans of Claverleigh, a house built less than twenty miles away at Creemore in 1871. Claverleigh was also a clergyman's house—built by the Reverend William R. Forster from plans drawn up by his brother, Richard, an English architect. Like The Cone, however, Claverleigh is board and batten, while the Rectory is stone. The Rectory has been altered somewhat over the years; a balcony has been removed, and the lower windows with their transoms and borders of small panes of coloured glass suggest changes in the 1890s. The asymmetric bay window, trusses in the gable, and deep eaves are characteristic of Gothic houses in Ontario, but its sophisticated complex of roof lines climbing progressively higher makes it rather exceptional.

51

53 St. Andrew's Presbyterian Church, Maple

Those who built this church of clapboard in 1862 were clearly influenced by fashionable Gothic Revival work in stone. The square entrance tower resembles a thinly-detailed masonry structure, complete with slender plank buttresses to either side, bracketed mouldings between the stages, and fretted corbelling above. Precisely because the church is made of wood, not stone, the dimensions of all the elements were reduced, producing a light, crisp quality. This superb piece of 'carpenter's Gothic' is topped by a spire of more solid, richer form.

54 St. Thomas' Church, Brooklin

St. Thomas' Anglican Church at Brooklin, built in 1870, provides a striking contrast with St. Andrew's Presbyterian Church at Maple. Instead of 'carpenter's Gothic' in clapboard, this church at Brooklin is built of board and batten in a sophisticated form of Gothic – an equivalent in wood for Tully's stone church at Lakefield (PLATE 27). The angular window-heads and tracery are a 'rational Gothic' accommodation to the peculiar property of wood: its straight, grainy quality makes arched or curving forms inappropriate. The spired bellcote is carried on a handsome system of braced posts deliberately exposed in a comparable demonstration of structural expression.

55 Former St. Andrew's Presbyterian Church, Byron Street South, Whitby

The old Presbyterian church in Whitby was begun in 1857 on an ambitious scale. It was opened in 1859, but the tall spire which was intended to complete the tower was never built. For the most part, St. Andrew's is built of red and yellow brick, even to the drip mouldings over the windows. The porch is of stone, however, and unusually rich by Presbyterian standards. In addition to a full range of Gothic Revival detailing, it features Scottish thistles, as well as English roses and Irish shamrocks, in the capitals to either side of the opening, and a bust of John Knox in high relief in the gable.

56   Board and batten house, Church Street, Elora

Board and batten houses were far more common than the number of those which survive intact would seem to indicate. Rarely as consistent in detailing as churches built of the same material, these board and batten houses mix elements like the Italianate entrance, the windows with Greek Revival heads, and the 'suicide door' in the gable with its eared jambs accompanying a pointed head surmounted by a Gothic label. The lacy, moulded and fretted bargeboards contrast very effectively with the ribbed texture of the walls. Such houses were meant to be seen, as here, in bright sunlight with strong shadows emphasizing the relief of the separate planes.

57   The Battel house, Spring Street, Cobourg

Broad dormers – or stilted gables – are a distinctive form found in Cobourg and the neighbouring parts of Northumberland County. In some cases, these dormers have a gambrel roof – a roof with two slopes on each side. Said to resemble a nun's coif, such dormers are, in fact, more like a wimple. In the Battel house, the sides of the dormers are straight and decorated with panelled pilasters. The fat ogee mouldings around the Gothic windows are another local form. The trim in the veranda (also typical of the area) is embellished with an entirely individual combination of quatrefoils, scrolls and hearts.

58   The Bentley house, Brougham

Few communities are dominated by a house, rather than a church or public building. But, in Brougham, this house, which stands where the Brock Road meets Highway 7, is the village landmark. It was built in 1853-55 by William Bentley, who had his patent medicine factory across the road. The house is large and remarkably detailed, with an extraordinary amalgam of varied features rising through the centre: the classicized entrance with free-standing columns, supplemented by a later porch with moulded square posts, the gothicized Palladian window with an elliptical head lifting the roof into a little gable, the patterned brick band under the eave and extending into the gable, the Italianate arcaded belvedere on the roof. Yet in spite of these assorted features, the result is a profoundly satisfying synthesis – 'a straightforward square house' in the Ontario tradition.

59 The Octagon, Port Hope

Polygonal houses are scattered through Ontario—usually not more than one in any locality. Port Hope has two examples: a small hexagonal cottage of brick, and this large, stuccoed octagonal house, which is one of the most satisfying examples in the province. Like so many Port Hope houses, it is built against a slope. As a result, the entrance and drawing-room were on the upper level, while the kitchen and dining-room were below. The house dates from 1856, when the Port Hope, Lindsay & Beaverton Railway was nearing completion. Apparently the house originally had a flat roof, which made the cupola seem nearly twice as tall; the substitution of a pitched roof has undoubtedly improved its appearance. Within, the rooms have curious but not unpleasing shapes, and there are two charming walnut staircases—one leading down to the kitchen and dining-room, and the other up to a gallery around the cupola.

60 Octagonal house, Main Street West, Picton

This attractive little octagon in Picton is more characteristic of such houses in Ontario, and of the smaller designs illustrated by Orson Squire Fowler, the New York phrenologist who promoted the octagonal fad. The walls are said to be constructed of 'grout'—lime mortar poured, like concrete, in forms—again reflecting Fowler's influence. The octagonal motif is extended through the veranda posts and chimney; the bay windows are of the usual form—which happens to be semi-octagonal.

61 Farmhouse, near Allisonville

This carefully-executed stone house of the mid-century is an 'Ontario cottage' from which the front veranda has been removed. The French doors to either side, which would have opened on the veranda, are set—like windows—in advance of the deeply-recessed doorway typical of the period; all are beautifully panelled to match. The monitor on the roof is not a belvedere, or viewing gallery, but an overhead lantern to light the sleeping-loft, a small upper floor concealed within the roof and reached by an enclosed stairway. A frame summer kitchen and shed form a picturesque extension to the side, in contrast with the formal regularity of the house.

62 The White house, Whitevale

Truman White, who built this house sometime between 1840 and 1845, gave his name to Whitevale – though the community was originally called Major or Majorville. It was once a small industrial village with a grist mill, sawmill, planing mill, cooperage and woollen factory; at one time all of these belonged to White, but all have gone, and only the houses built in the days of Whitevale's prosperity remain. The clapboard White house is typical of smaller houses in growing centres in the 1840s in turning its gable end to the road. The house is extraordinarily well-preserved; its lean-to is an appealing, asymmetric addition which balances the offset Classic doorway.

63 Farmhouse, near Stouffville

It was the custom of the Mennonites to build a 'doddy house' for the old people – 'grossdoddy' and 'grossmummy.' The doddy house customarily projects to the front edge of the veranda of the main house, and has its own entrance from this shared veranda, although it also has an internal connection with the larger house. It was commonly two storeys, with its own stairway, and had a chimney for a box stove. Being built a generation later than the main house, it usually differed in material and detail: here, the mid-Victorian main house is a particularly fine example of patterned brick – with small windows under the eaves (more characteristic of the houses of German settlers in southwestern Ontario) – while the later Victorian doddy house is of V-jointed vertical boarding (a material nearly peculiar to the Markham-Pickering area). A few feet away (to the right in the photo) stands another house, a clapboard structure of much earlier date – c. 1810 – and a smoke-house.

64 Veranda of house on Mill Street, Elora

This elaborate veranda, with its fretwork and bell-cast roof carried on curved rafters, contrasts strongly with the simple form favoured by the Mennonites, as in the farmhouse near Stouffville. The veranda provided a covered and slightly elevated place for exercise in bad weather. The example on this amply-proportioned house at Elora is deeper than usual, and more useful for sitting out than most. Tall French doors open onto this veranda, which encloses both the southern and western sides of the house.

65 St. Mark's Rectory, Byron Street, Niagara-on-the-Lake

Built in 1858, the Rectory is an attractive example of an Italianate villa. The mode, inspired by villas in north-central Italy—especially as reflected in sixteenth and seventeenth-century painting—was introduced in Britain for small suburban houses at the beginning of the nineteenth century. In the 1840s and 1850s houses 'in the Italian style' were featured in American pattern books. The Rectory is typical in that it is L-shaped and has a square tower, containing the entrance, within the angle. The few round-headed windows and deep eaves with widely-spaced brackets are also characteristic, but the later date of this example is suggested by the height of both the individual storeys and the tower. The porch has been renewed.

66 Victoria Hall, King Street, Cobourg

The cornerstone of Victoria Hall was laid in December 1856. The building, incorporating the town hall, court house, and masonic hall, was officially opened by the Prince of Wales in September 1860. It was designed by Kivas Tully and, in some ways, appears to challenge St. Lawrence Hall in Toronto, built in 1850 by Tully's leading rival, William Thomas. Victoria Hall, however, gains greatly from being set back behind the street line so that the sharp modelling of the fine-grained stone—from Cleveland, Ohio—shows to advantage, even though the building faces north. The grouping of the windows down the length of the facade and the stratified appearance of the strongly-banded storeys make the building seem extraordinarily large, even on the site—until the scale of the cupola is appreciated. The restrained eclecticism of this Victorian Classical building makes it one of the finest expressions of the nineteenth century in the province.

67 House and store, Camden East

This store is to Camden East what Victoria Hall is to Cobourg. Built of stone at about the same time as Victoria Hall, located at the crossroads, and the most impressive building in the village, it documents Anna Jameson's comment in *Winter Studies and Summer Rambles* (1837) that 'the grocery store, or general shop ... in a new Canadian village is always the best house in the place.'

68 Old St. Lawrence Hotel, Walton Street, Port Hope

The large block known both as the St. Lawrence Hotel and St. Lawrence Hall was built in 1858. It is much larger than it appears in this view (looking south from Cavan Street): ten bays are shown, but seven extend farther to the left. Because Walton Street slopes, no two of the ground-floor shops are at the same level, their tall windows present a stepped appearance, and the cast-iron piers vary considerably in length. The hotel proper is a markedly attenuated version of the Italianate style, and contrasts pleasantly with the Classic blocks on the same street of only a half-dozen years before (PLATE 1). The facade has been carefully restored; where the ornamental iron supports had been removed, they were recast, but some of the smaller detailing in the cast-iron window heads has not been replaced and their pendants have been removed.

69 Commercial blocks, King Street West, Dundas

This photograph shows part of a series of connected commercial blocks, built after a fire in 1880. The old hardware store preserves its interior fittings and elements like the attractively-panelled doors, which rarely survive. The double block to the right was essentially the same originally. To the left of the hardware store there is a plainer block, the windows of which were not encrusted with the wooden mouldings, pressed metal and cast-iron trim that make the other units so memorable.

70 Dundas cotton factory, Main Street, Dundas

One of the earliest cotton mills in this province was established in 1858 by Joseph Wright on Spencer's Creek at Main Street, Dundas. In 1867, when he was offering shares in his successful enterprise, it had become a large complex powered by two steam engines in addition to water power. The photograph shows the elaborately-decorated facade, with walls of white brick. The lower row of columns, the faces of the corner piers, the cornice of the main storey, the upper window heads and sills, and the acanthus-decorated capitals of the pilasters, all were of cast iron. The in-filling of the ground-floor front was a later alteration, and here the windows and surrounds were stone; the wooden balustrade was also a later alteration, replacing the pediment of a gable roof which was removed. This historic mill was demolished in 1974.

71 Lennox & Addington County Court House, Thomas Street, Napanee

This Court House was begun in 1864, and the first court was held here on 25 October, 1865. The building is markedly original, a reworking in Italianate style of a much earlier Georgian type. The upper floor, with its tall, round-arched windows, houses the courtroom. The whole building is set off dramatically by the stilted, arched portico with its paired, slender piers. The square wooden cupola adds remarkably to its presence: by contrast with the clock tower of Victoria Hall in Cobourg, which tends to reduce the apparent size of that delicately-detailed building, the slender and flat detailing of the cupola here, and its relatively small windows, augment the building's grandeur.

72 Town Hall, Caledonia

Caledonia was incorporated as a village in 1853, and its Town Hall built four years later at a cost of £800. The building demonstrates the blunt show of power, as well as the restless love of variation, characteristic of so much Victorian architecture. The Hall resembles a brass-bound box with its massive banding around the edges—especially in the forceful, paired orders at either side of the main front, and the heavy-looking entablature around the gable. Typically, the detail is concentrated in areas and consciously modified from one to another, as in the entrance and the grouped windows.

73 Town Hall, Gore Street, Perth

The Town Hall, dated 1863, illustrates clearly the mid-Victorian trend toward Italianate handling imposed on a classic block. Nearly all buildings in this manner freely combine elements drawn from very disparate Renaissance sources. Typical of the 1860s are the highly-textured vermiculated stones (resembling worm-eaten wood) used in the trim, including the rusticated bands in the pilasters of the doorway. Equally characteristic of the period are the stilted windows on the ground floor — arched windows with a raised segmental head — and the peculiar variant of the Palladian window in the centre, with all the openings round-headed. Though only a two-storey building, the Town Hall has stunning impact and remains — appropriately — the pivotal building on Perth's main street.

74 *The William Mirick house, Merrickville*

William Mirick, the founder of Merrickville, built this house on the north bank of the Rideau in the second quarter of the nineteenth century. In 1869 the property was bought from the Merrick family by William Pearson, owner of the foundry which can be seen at the extreme right of the photograph. The present house appears to be a thorough renovation about this time. The substantial quality of the detail in this handsome house is suggested by the massive gateposts at the foot of the sweeping drive, and the gate to the footpath that once bordered it. In the gate alone, the width of the rails and the flat treatment of the stiles, the chamfering of the braces and the positioning of the palings edgewise are indicative of a date in the 1860s or 1870s.

75 *Jakes Block, Merrickville*

This L-shaped commercial block, sited at the major crossroads in Merrickville, is surprisingly large – big enough to invite comparison with the neighbouring mills (PLATE 35). It was built by Eleazar Whitmarsh in the late 1860s, and sold to Samuel Jakes in 1871. The positioning of the windows in this view suggests the unusual height of each storey. From this rear aspect, the building appears very traditional: an arched carriageway gives access to the yard from the street; the end walls are nearly windowless, as the block extends to the property line, while thick party walls with parapets above the roof and paired chimneys divide the building into separate units to prevent the spread of fire.

76 *Jakes Block, Merrickville*

The street faces of the building in the previous plate present a strikingly different appearance. The second-floor windows are longer, and the ground floor is treated as a large, continuous arcade. The surface of the building is connected by a network of horizontal and vertical bands, more heavily rusticated than the rest of the masonry. The eaves and the upper part of the wall are also strongly textured. The huge sheet of curved glass in the rounded corner is a replacement, made about the turn of the century, and the stained-glass transoms in the adjacent ground-floor windows point to other alterations about the same time.

77 Lanark County Jail, Beckwith Street, Perth

By comparison with the contemporary Town Hall (PLATE 73), Perth Jail—built in 1862-63—is so brusque and coarse as to make the former seem almost bland. The walls of the Jail are dressed with rock-faced masonry. The few openings in its face are trimmed with the wide bands of smooth stone favoured from the mid-century for penal institutions in Ontario; the window heads particularly, with their boldly-cut keystones, seem to grip the sash with the bite of a vise. The ramped entrance gives access below to the cells, and manages to combine the imagery of a bridge of sighs and a traitors' gate.

78 Lennox & Addington County Registry Office, Thomas Street, Napanee

The Napanee Registry Office was built in 1871-72 on the standard plan drawn up by the Department of Public Works in 1868. These buildings are roughly twice as wide and three times as long as they are high—very direct and pleasing proportions. The interior consists of three brick-vaulted spaces running from side to side. The exterior, usually of brick but sometimes stone, permitted some range in detailing; in this instance a blind arcade with stone capitals frames the round-headed openings. To help make these buildings as fireproof as possible, cast iron was used for the name plate, window heads, sills and door. Regrettably, the original door shown here was replaced in 1972.

79 Schoolhouse, Cedar Grove

Tenders were solicited 'for building a Brick School House in SS 20, Markham' in February 1869, to replace a frame building, and the school is dated the same year on the tablet in the gable. The front door was for visitors and the teacher; unusually, the pupils entered this school through a pair of doors at the rear. White brick is used to outline the openings and all the edges of the building, and is also laid anglewise—a band of imbrication—across the face. The repetition of round-arched openings, in the door, the windows, the vent and the belfry, produces a bouncy rhythm in this otherwise strongly rectilinear design. Now used as a community hall, this is possibly the most handsome and most completely preserved red-brick schoolhouse surviving in the province.

80 All Saints Church and schoolhouse, Dundas Street West, Whitby

A simple stone church, St. John's, was built by the Anglicans in Port Whitby in 1846 — and still stands — but in 1864 the Deanery of East York noted that this was 'about a mile and a quarter from the Kingston Road, on which is situated the now rising town of Whitby. Whatever it may have been once, this church is not now the right thing, or in the right place.' As a result, All Saints' was built in 1865-66, on the Kingston Road in the town of Whitby proper, two blocks west of the centre. Designed by Gundry & Langley, who specialized in church architecture of the 'right' sort, All Saints' is characteristic of Anglican churches in this period: built of red brick with yellow trim, it is broad and very high, with a tall spire on the asymmetric tower. By 1870, when Henry Langley designed the schoolhouse, the bolder effect of striped brickwork was in vogue.

81 Schoolhouse and Free Methodist Church, Harrowsmith

In their architecture, nonconformist denominations often maintained a profile literally lower than the High Church world of many Anglican congregations, as comparison of this plate with the previous one makes clear. Yet some architectural predilections of the Anglican communion carry over: two colours of limestone are very systematically employed to produce a banded appearance in both the schoolhouse and the Methodist Church in Harrowsmith. Some referred to such effects as 'permanent polychromy,' whether the pattern was achieved by using different colours of brick, as at Whitby, or stone as here; others called this 'streaky bacon style.'

82 Former Methodist Church, Whitevale

Whitevale is a loosely-planned community strung out along the fifth concession of Pickering. The road descends from the White house on the west side (PLATE 62), to West Duffin's Creek where the mills were once clustered, then climbs to a still-higher level on the east side. The Methodist Church, built in 1884, stands toward the crest, but is set back from the road behind some spruce. Effective use is made of a series of broad gables filled with stepped brickwork — corbel tables — in both the end of the nave and the porch of highly individual form. The rose in the gable, like all the other windows, is surrounded by a tough, cog-like pattern of brick.

83 Business blocks, Walton Street, Port Hope

Little more than twenty years separate the early and late Victorian blocks on Walton Street; this group contains examples of both. The offices of the *Evening Guide* have been restored to suggest their appearance when built shortly before 1850. Next to them, at the larger scale characteristic of later nineteenth-century architecture, and breaking the roof line of all the older buildings with its tall mansard roof, is what was once Russell's Cabinet Warehouse. This dates from the early 1870s. The corner building was originally Molson's Bank, and was nearly uniform with the store between it and Russell's.

84 Penman's No. 1 Mill, West River Street, Paris

John Penman purchased the property here in 1868; in 1874 he built this fine mill overlooking the Nith River. It is part of a large complex, most of which is considerably later in date than this building. It is a typical mill structure, with wooden columns supporting the heavy wooden beams which carry the floors. On two floors, the columns have been replaced with cast iron. The external walls, which are load-bearing, are strengthened by piers; those down the long sides of the building support the internal beams. The mansard roof with dormers is typical of the period; this one has a central monitor which, however, does not give much light and was probably required for ventilation. The structure is enhanced by its attractive windows with hoods of brick. This is functional architecture of the nineteenth century at its best.

85 Riverside Terrace, Hespeler

Good examples of workers' housing, like this attractive row of local stone, are rare in Ontario. In fact, this type of housing is unusual in this province; its place was taken by the small labourers' cottages common to both towns and villages—and found even in the cities. The repetition of uniform porches and evenly-spaced windows gives the complex a regularity reminiscent of industrial buildings. But the generous proportions throughout contrast with the meanness of working-class housing elsewhere at the time. These houses were built by Jacob Hespeler about 1864, to serve as accommodation for workers in his nearby mill.

86 Dundurn, near Waterford

Certain kinds of houses, like this farmhouse at the hamlet which takes its name from the house, are as characteristic of urban areas as of rural. Farmhouses are frequently larger than urban houses, but the latter are often more elaborately detailed. The considerable height of both storeys of this farmhouse is obvious from a comparison of the paired front windows with the tall front door. The mortar joints in the fieldstone are particularly rough – even by rural standards. On the other hand, Dundurn is unusual in the rich treatment of the porch, doorway and eaves. The latter sport a wonderful array of brackets with turned pendants.

87 House, Queen Street, Kincardine

The more refined stonework marks this house as an urban example of the familiar, later nineteenth-century Ontario house. A narrow, projecting centre with a shallow gable – or pediment – but deep eaves on a hip-roofed block are the distinguishing features of the type. The paired brackets of especially complex form under the eaves suggest a date in the 1870s for this example. In its general effect, the rich (and strangely-assorted) treatment of the stone trim recalls the opulence of some Italianate commercial buildings of the previous decade. Few houses of this type demonstrate such vigour.

88 House, Wellington Street South, Goderich

This house, at the corner of West Street, probably built in the seventies or early eighties, is decidedly advanced in fashion. With its studied silhouette, composition and ornament, it could vie with the better houses of the same period in any Ontario city. Like many 'French Renaissance' houses, it is uncommonly tall, puts the front in the narrow end, throws big bays asymmetrically to either side, and has a mansard-roofed corner tower. The trim is consistent on all sides, but increases in intricacy level by level. It is a remarkably unaltered example of late nineteenth-century eclecticism, invention and ostentation – the quintessential Victorian house. The type is more common in many parts of the United States than in Ontario, but a delightful and significant art form wherever it occurs.

89   *House, Union Street, Picton*

Some details of the house shown here suggest a date in the late 1860s or early 1870s – the segmental window heads, the paired lights in the sash, and the paired, lozenge-panelled doors fitted under a round head. But some of the turned and fretted ornament incorporated in the porch seems more in line with the 1880s. The shape of the house overall suggests a still later date, in the closing decade of the century: it is nearly a cube, with the entrance tucked into an indented portion of the front, and low, hipped roofs covering the whole. The cast-iron railing looks earlier than the woodwork below it, but this can be explained by the fact that moulds once made continued to be used for many years.

90   *Fire Hall, Meaford*

Built to the design of a local architect, James A. Ellis, in 1887, this fire hall represents one of the new types of building that appeared in the nineteenth century as public services increased. Tall, wide doors were required for the apparatus and a tall, slender tower for drawing up the canvas hoses to dry. The upper stage of the tower was rebuilt in its present form in 1908. The use of especially-large, round-arched openings is characteristic of the late 1880s and the 1890s. The fully-developed Romanesque Revival, with massive trim in carved stone and moulded brick, is rare outside Toronto, but is approached here in the overall effect of juxtaposed large and small openings and even in detailing like the arcaded corbelling in the parapet. The whole design is well co-ordinated and has a modest dignity.

91   *Row houses, Byron Street North, Whitby*

In this example of row housing of the late-nineteenth century, white brick quoins, flush with the face, are used to distinguish the units, while a white band with recessed cruciform ornament – long popular east of Toronto – ties all into one row. The three units to the left were identical until the handsome enclosed porch was pulled off the middle one. The fourth unit differs in carrying the bay window through two floors, and the fifth is a mirror image of any of the first three, so that a cadence of forms is created in this modest but attractive and still very urban architecture.

92   *Railway station, Stouffville*

Stouffville station was built for the Toronto & Nipissing Railway, which had the distinction of being 'the first narrow [3 feet 6 inch] gauge railway opened for traffic on the continent of America.' Service was inaugurated on 12 July, 1871 between Toronto and Uxbridge; in 1872 it was completed to Coboconk, the nearest it ever got to Lake Nipissing. The station almost certainly dates from the earliest days of the railway, but from a map of 1875 it would appear that the long, low freight shed has been substantially extended. The waiting-room fills the near end of the station; the projecting telegrapher's bay gives a clear view of the line and, incidentally, enriches the building's profile.

93   *Textile mill, Campbellford*

About 1856 a dam was built across the Trent River at Campbellford to create a power source for a number of mills. In 1881 the Trent Valley Woolen Manufacturing Company built this imposing factory. As at Penman's No. 1 Mill in Paris, its simple brick piers and corbelling are not purely decorative, but functional elements which serve to stiffen the walls. The piers help to carry the loads of the laminated floor beams, which are also supported inside the building by surprisingly slender turned wooden columns. The use of wood for the columns is unusual in so large a factory at this late date, when cast iron was generally used for the purpose. The chimney stack and elevator penthouse are part of the original mill.

94   *Campbell flour mill, Campbellford*

The right-hand portion of this fine brick mill was built in 1883, the date recorded in the gable of the hoistway. The steeply-pitched mansard roof resembles those used in houses of the period, while projecting piers and corbelling at the eaves emphasize the equally strong form and unusual height of the rest of the building. To judge by the slightly increased amount of ornament in their dormers, the blank-walled portion of the building to the left was an addition soon after the part with the hoist was built. The internal structure is similar to that of the textile mill in the preceding photograph, but with slightly stouter proportions in the turned wooden posts, heavy hewn beams and closely-spaced joists designed to carry immense loads of grain and flour.

95 Water Street, St. Mary's

This fine stone row, probably dating from the 1860s, is dominated by the former Opera House, completed in 1880 for the Odd Fellows, whose meeting rooms occupied the top floor. The Opera House itself was on the second floor, with stores below. According to the local newspaper, the inaugural performance by a travelling company, 8 October, 1880, was 'redeemed only by the festive spirit of the occasion.' At a later performance the same year, both lighting and heating systems failed. This inauspicious start presaged the sale of the building in 1904 and its conversion to a harness factory. Some years later it was again converted – this time to its most recent function as a flour mill. In spite of its curious history, the incomparable Gothic Revival facade has remained virtually unchanged; the central 'peak' has been removed – all but the finial – leaving half a roundel in the stonework (evidently intended at one time for a clock face).

96 Queen Street, St. Mary's

The elaborate watch-making and jewelry establishment of William Andrews dominates this block – and almost the whole length – of Queen Street, illustrating the tendency to competition among buildings in Victorian architecture. Only the tall tower of the much later municipal building, near the top of this rising main street, challenges the jeweler's lofty and eye-catching mansard with its clock tower. The frankly-variegated detail is piquant and arresting among the more conventionally-detailed Victorian blocks – one of which was refaced to make the new Royal Bank premises without destroying the street's profile, scale and distinctive round-headed detailing.

97 Main Street, Seaforth

All the structures seen in this photograph were built following the destruction of the business district by a fire in 1877, just two years after Seaforth became a town. They are typical of later nineteenth-century Ontario, and their modesty helps to maintain a pleasing unity achieved by simple devices like the common eaves (not dictated by the window heights) and the use of common materials (white brick). While the unity is marked, there is nothing approaching uniformity in the lively and changeful surface patterns. Just one building, the Cardo Block of 1879, rises above the others.

98 Groves Block, St. David and St. Andrew Streets, Fergus

It is most regrettable that this corner block, built in 1880, was largely demolished in 1972. Apart from the fact that nineteenth-century banks—a special architectural genre—have almost entirely vanished, few later Victorian buildings in Ontario were so individualistic. The hooded Gothic dormers and turrets almost obscured the heavy mansard roof. It was this playful treatment of the upper storey that gave the building its distinction and relieved the heavy handling of the stonework. The Groves Block provided the town's major intersection with a handsome focus—now lost.

99 Mill Street, Almonte

The old Post Office of 1890 dominates the winding street, part of the very irregular layout of the centre of Almonte, a small mill town which developed around the falls on the Mississippi River. The community grew rapidly in the 1850s with the opening of several woollen mills, and was given further impetus when in 1859 it became the northern terminus of the Brockville & Ottawa Railway (later extended some twenty miles north to Sand Point, on the Ottawa River). Almonte was incorporated as a village in 1871, and as a town ten years later. The Post Office is in Thomas Fuller's distinctive manner; the heavy, rock-faced stonework and the elaborate patterning of the window heads and gables are typical of his style. In spite of a family resemblance among the many public buildings—particularly post offices and customs houses—which he designed as Dominion Architect, almost every one conveys a sense of both its time and place.

LIST OF PLATES

1. Walton Street, Port Hope, looking west from the bridge
2. The White House, near Amherstview
3. Log house, Palmer Street, Guelph
4. The White Chapel, on Highway 49 north of Picton
5. The Macpherson house, Thomas Street, Napanee
6. The Spencer house, Spencer Street East, Cobourg
7. The Barnum house, on Highway 2 west of Grafton
8. The Webster house, King Street West, Cobourg
9. The Wilderness, King Street, Niagara-on-the-Lake
10. House, Gage Street, Niagara-on-the-Lake
11. Doorway, Breakenridge house, Mississauga Street, Niagara-on-the-Lake
12. Houses on Queen Street, Niagara-on-the-Lake
13. Roslyn Cottage, Queen Street, Niagara-on-the-Lake
14. St. Andrew's Presbyterian Church, Niagara-on-the-Lake
15. The Peck house, Dibble Street West, Prescott
16. The Alpheus Jones house, Dibble Street West, Prescott
17. Old Victoria College, from College Street, Cobourg
18. Terrace, Walton Street, Port Hope
19. Bluestone, Dorset Street East, Port Hope
20. St. Andrew's Presbyterian Church, Colborne
21. Huron County Jail, Goderich
22. Prince Edward County Buildings, Picton
23. Old Church of St. Mary Magdalene, Picton
24. The Newburgh Academy, Newburgh
25. Former Grammar School, Williamstown
26. Holy Trinity Anglican Church, Chippawa
27. St. Andrew's Presbyterian Church, Williamstown
28. Riverest, L'Orignal
29. Baltimore Hotel, Division Street, Cobourg
30. Inge-Va, Craig Street, Perth
31. The Matheson house, Gore Street East, Perth
32. St. John's Roman Catholic Church, from Brock Street, Perth
33. View on Gore Street, Perth
34. Gore Street and bridge over the Little River, Perth
35. Mills, Merrickville
36. Farmhouse, near Easton's Corners
37. Mennonite Church, Altona
38. Bethel Chapel, Britannia Road, near Kilbride
39. Store building, Martintown
40. Store and house, Waterdown
41. Porch, Lynnwood, Simcoe
42. The Sowden house, Burwell and Church Streets, Paris
43. The Sovereign house, Waterford
44. Town Hall, Dundas
45. Bruce Street Public School, Milton
46. United Church, Actinolite
47. Christ Church, Lakefield
48. Former Grand Trunk Railway station, Shannonville
49. The Tracey house, Church Street, St. Mary's
50. Pinehurst, Pine Street, Port Hope
51. The Cone, Dorset Street West, Port Hope
52. The Rectory, Ontario Street, Collingwood
53. St. Andrew's Presbyterian Church, Maple
54. St. Thomas' Church, Brooklin
55. Former St. Andrew's Presbyterian Church, Byron Street South, Whitby
56. Board and batten house, Church Street, Elora
57. The Battel house, Spring Street, Cobourg
58. The Bentley house, Brougham
59. The Octagon, Port Hope
60. Octagonal house, Main Street West, Picton
61. Farmhouse, near Allisonville
62. The White house, Whitevale
63. Farmhouse, near Stouffville
64. Veranda of house on Mill Street, Elora
65. St. Mark's Rectory, Byron Street, Niagara-on-the-Lake
66. Victoria Hall, King Street, Cobourg
67. House and store, Camden East
68. Old St. Lawrence Hotel, Walton Street, Port Hope
69. Commercial blocks, King Street West, Dundas
70. Dundas cotton factory, Main Street, Dundas
71. Lennox & Addington County Court House, Thomas Street, Napanee
72. Town Hall, Caledonia
73. Town Hall, Gore Street, Perth
74. The William Mirick house, Merrickville
75. Jakes Block, Merrickville
76. Jakes Block, Merrickville
77. Lanark County Jail, Beckwith Street, Perth
78. Lennox & Addington County Registry Office, Thomas Street, Napanee
79. Schoolhouse, Cedar Grove
80. All Saints Church and schoolhouse, Dundas Street West, Whitby
81. Schoolhouse and Free Methodist Church, Harrowsmith
82. Former Methodist Church, Whitevale
83. Business blocks, Walton Street, Port Hope
84. Penman's No. 1 Mill, West River Street, Paris
85. Riverside Terrace, Hespeler
86. Dundurn, near Waterford
87. House, Queen Street, Kincardine
88. House, Wellington Street South, Goderich
89. House, Union Street, Picton
90. Fire Hall, Meaford
91. Row houses, Byron Street North, Whitby
92. Railway station, Stouffville
93. Textile mill, Campbellford
94. Campbell flour mill, Campbellford
95. Water Street, St. Mary's
96. Queen Street, St. Mary's
97. Main Street, Seaforth
98. Groves Block, St. David and St. Andrew Streets, Fergus
99. Mill Street, Almonte

Copyright © 1974 by Oberon Press

All rights reserved: no part of this book may be reproduced in any form or by any means, electronic or mechanical, except by a reviewer, who may quote brief passages in a review to be printed in a newspaper or magazine or broadcast on radio or television.

Library of Congress Card No. 74-76153

ISBN 0 88750 130 3

Edited by Gail Low, designed by Michael Macklem and printed in Canada from plates prepared at the Coach House Press by Stan Bevington.

PUBLISHED IN CANADA BY OBERON PRESS

FIGURES IN THE TEXT

1 Parsonage House, Yorkshire, from Isaac Ware, *A Complete Body of Architecture*, 1756
2 First Settler's Shanty in Palmerston, C.W. from a stereograph taken in the 1860s by J.W. Love (Ontario Archives)
3 The Priory, Guelph, as a railway station, from an early twentieth-century photograph (*Globe and Mail*, Toronto)
4 Design for a Dwelling House for Chas. Jones Esq., Weston, 1854, by Kivas Tully (Fisher Library, University of Toronto)
5 The MacMartin house, Perth, from a daguerrotype, c. 1850 (Ontario Archives)
6 Illustrations of farmhouses from *Canada Farmer* (*lower*, 16 May, 1864; *upper*, 15 April, 1865)
7 Plan and Elevation of a Church from Asher Benjamin, *The American Builder's Companion*, 1827
8 Church of Ireland parish church, Kilternan, Co. Dublin, by John Semple, from the *Dublin Penny Journal*, 19 January, 1833
9 Architects' design for Wesleyan Methodist Church, Aylmer, Quebec, 1874, by Langley, Langley & Burke (Ontario Archives)
10 Rejected design for Newcastle District Court House, Cobourg, 1828, by James G. Chewett (Ontario Archives)
11 Halton County Court House, Milton, from Tremaine's *Map of the County of Halton*, 1858
12 Huron County Court House, Goderich, from the *Canadian Illustrated News*, 19 August, 1871
13 Plan of the Town of Goderich, Upper Canada, 1829 (Ontario Archives)
14 Design for Rural School House, from the *Journal of Education*, March 1873 (republished in J. George Hodgins, *The School House*, 1876)
15 Architect's design for the Post Office, Port Hope, 1882, by Thomas Fuller (Department of Public Works, Ottawa)
16 View at Napanee, c. 1830-40, by Thomas Burrowes (Ontario Archives)
17 Railway station at Hochst, Germany, from Rowland Macdonald Stephenson, *Railways: An Introductory Sketch*, 1850
18 Diagram of a 'utilitarian building' from James Fergusson, *The Illustrated Handbook of Architecture*, 1859
19 Victoria Buildings, Bowmanville, from Tremaine's *Map of the County of Durham*, 1861
20 View of Oshawa, C.W., c. 1841-46
21 View on Walton Street, Port Hope, from Tremaine's *Map of the County of Durham*, 1861
22 Royal Bank and remnant of Groves Block, Fergus, 1973
23 Panorama of Port Hope from a series of photographs taken c. 1880 (Ontario Archives)